Be Still &
Be Quiet

R. Mikki Addison

ARCHWAY
PUBLISHING

Archway Publishing books may be ordered through booksellers or by contacting:

Archway Publishing
1663 Liberty Drive
Bloomington, IN 47403
www.archwaypublishing.com
1 (888) 242-5904

ISBN: 978-1-4808-7228-8 (sc)
ISBN: 978-1-4808-7227-1 (e)

Library of Congress Control Number: 2018914073

Print information available on the last page.

Archway Publishing rev. date: 08/21/2019

Contents

About This Book

I have decided that *Be Still & Be Quiet* will be an instructor and advisor. This is not a movement but a concept. It is unorthodox and a different approach to writing a book, but different is often better.

Be Still & Be Quiet teaches parents and other caregivers of children how to instill in their children respect, discipline, self-control, independence, consideration for others, empathy, and self-determination so they can become the leaders of tomorrow.

Be Still & Be Quiet is for parents, grandparents, foster parents, adoptive parents, godparents, and relatives who need to visit for the first time or those of the older generation who need to revisit old school family values. It is a reminder for all parents that there was a time when children learned to be respectful and obedient to their parents and all elders. A time when children were eager to be helpful and had positive attitudes about their families. Children were appreciative of the good life they were living. Children were happy! Parents knew happiness and taught their children to be happy and grateful. Frequently a "Gratitude Journal" was made by the children who simply folded several blank pages of paper, put two staples in the middle, and added the title on the front page. Walla!

Be Still & Be Quiet focuses on advising, suggesting, and instructing all who care for children to develop an understanding of and form relationships with their children. Parents need to realize that it is better to have control over your children rather than to let them get so out of control that outside authority have to discipline your children for you.

In *Be Still & Be Quiet*, my personal experiences are the experiences of minority Mothers all over the world. We raise our daughters and love our sons. This means our daughters are usually strong willed, logical, and purposeful in life. Our sons are not as fortunate. It is well documented that systems purposely erect barriers to hinder if not completely stop them from obtaining success. We are fearful for our sons' safety every time they walk out the door. Our sons are frequently raised in single households by Mothers who no matter how hard they try to wear two hats cannot teach their sons to be men.

All over the United States in the public school system, law enforcement, the district attorney's office, the courts, and the prison systems that warehouse minority males, minorities are treated harsher and often more unjustly in comparison to Caucasian males. These systems are designed to be unforgiving of minority males' offenses against society.

Frequently by the time they are preteens or teens, our sons have become disenchanted, frustrated, confused, angry, lost, and depressed. For close to fifteen years, I worked at the Fresno County Jail and the Fresno County Juvenile Justice Campus (JJC) as a mental health counselor for Fresno's Behavioral Health Department. I have witnessed the unequal and unjust incarceration of this targeted minority population of men and boys. I hope this horrendous state of affairs will end sooner rather than later.

Chapters are directed at parents raising their child or children; but, grandparent, foster parents, godparents, adoptive parents, relatives, and anyone raising a child is to be substituted in its place.

All biblical quotes within this book are from the King James Version of the bible.

Instead of saying, "Your child this" and "Your child that," I have chosen to at times insert a child's name, possibly your child's name. If not, you may want to substitute your child's name to personalize the lesson, the situation, or counseling given.

I have decided to not use the phrase "he/she"; instead, I made chapters gender friendly and talk about a male, your son; or, a female, your daughter.

You will find several mantras throughout this book. A mantra is a sacred utterance, a sound, a syllable, a philosophical statement, or a group of words some people believe have psychological and spiritual power. The spiritual value of a mantra comes when it is audible, visible, or present in thought. It is best to post mantras on the refrigerator and recite them daily. A mantra is similar to an affirmation or a prayer. Therefore, it is good to start every morning by reciting one or two mantras.

This is my vision. It has been this way from the beginning. I never intended to interject myself into this, my first book. I never wanted to say, "I did this or I did that," nor did I want to sprinkle anecdotes here and there.

If you believe there are contradictions in *Be Still & Be Quiet*, please note that I wrote this book over a period of several years. *Be Still & Be Quiet* is not based on empirical evidence but on my professional experience as a social worker and mental health counselor. Additionally, it is based on my personal experiences as the Mother of a daughter and a son, who are now adults, along with several grandchildren and two great grandchildren.

This book is dedicated to my parents

Julia Hillard-McIntosh-Brown
Amsie McIntosh
Nathaniel Brown, Sr.

A special thank you to my other Mother and Father

Ruth Proffit
Luther Henry

A special thank you to my hero & Father figure

Woodrow Moreau Sr.

Thank you to my children

Heather L. Addison
Charles T. Addison, Jr.

Thank you to my brother and sister-in-law

Percy and Rosina McIntosh

Thank you to my daughter-in-law
Cristina Bush-Addison

Thank you to my four grandchildren

Dejanae' Addison
Aniyah Addison
Alayah Addison
Asanti Addison

Thank you to my two great grandchildren

Thank you to family and friends who
made donations to my dream.
Thank you to my many manuscript readers and editors.

Acknowledgements

Illustrator
CURTIS O'NEIL

Graphic Designer
PRASADAM UZCATEGUI

In Remembrance

Darryl Rene Hilliard, Jr. – Cousin
August 30 1983 – June 15, 2004

Nathaniel Anthony Brown, Jr. – Step-Brother
August 6, 1955 –July 9, 2005

Michael Brice Daniels - Cousin
February 23, 1990 – February 19, 2017

Daran Adams Jackson - Cousin
March 16, 1995 – October 22, 2017

"It's time for us as a people to start makin some changes.
Let's change the way we eat,
Let's change the way we live,
And, let's change the way we treat each other."

Tupac Shakur
6/16/71 – 9/13/96

Chapter 1

Be Still & Be Quiet is an exciting, opinionated, straight-talking, self-help guide to parenting by practicing love, discipline, and consistency.

Be Still & Be Quiet Is Opinionated

This book is not evidenced based or proven fact. I developed this opinionated parental guideline to help people overcome negative and problematic behavior in their children. If a child or adolescent is out of control, poor parenting is primarily at fault. Establish and maintain family roles by identifying the proper hierarchy, "Who is the parent and who is the child?" is the idea behind *Be Still & Be Quiet*. If your child has been in charge and allowed to run amuck, that is a problem, but hopefully its solution is in this book.

Why today's children cannot be still and be quiet? The answer is simple. They can be still and quiet if they are taught to be so starting at age one or two. No preschooler can be still and quiet if he has never been taught. If his parents have instead begged him to be good, promised things, bartered with him, let him do as he pleased, and asked what he wanted to do. They in essence have given him the power to make his own decisions.

Be Still & Be Quiet will assist parents, grandparents, adoptive parents, foster parents, and guardians to develop skills essential to nurture their children into open-minded, independent thinkers who are compassionate, reverent to their elders, and of good character and citizenship. Compassion means, "Suffering with others." Parents developing skills will happen in part by addressing negative behaviors early in their children's growth and development. Its purpose is to correct oppositional-defiant behavior before it is a problem. Moreover, it is about having a healthy household with loving parents who respect each other and have a trusting relationship with their children. *Be Still & Be Quiet* is not meant for parents who are mentally challenged or for parenting mentally challenged or mentally ill children.

> *Change will not come if we wait for some other person or some other time. We are the ones we've been waiting for. We are the change that we seek.*
>
> —Barack Obama

Chapter 2

Be Still & Be Quiet Is No-Nonsense

Be Still & Be Quiet is a no-nonsense parenting style versus one that emphasizes individualism or equal rights for children. This model incorporates specific household roles as well as rules. The adult male and female in the home are the parents. Their offspring are their children. Thus you have the roles of parent and child. Parents stand for authority as in "We are in charge" all the time, not sometimes, not a little bit, not until their children become teenagers or young adults. The role of a parent is that of teacher, nurturer, provider, and protector of his or her children while they live in the home. Even during college or after marriage, children are to respect their parents and treat them with the utmost courtesy.

For way too long, being in control of your children has been unthinkable. Who made it so? Professionals have swung the pendulum so far to the extreme left that your child became an uncontrollable and unbearable person in a quest for individuality, equality, and personhood. The psychological and therapeutic beliefs and principles are that we all have choices. Really? But does a two, three, or even six year old need choices? Will she be emotionally damaged if she doesn't have choices? *Be Still & Be Quiet* thinks not. Children are not the equals of adults. Toddlers and preschoolers cannot handle too much freedom of expression, too many choices, and decision making.

To all parents, know your role when parenting. Do not become confused by experts on the theory of the family system. Should you become confused, you will, without a doubt, have a kindergartner telling you and her new teacher at school what she will or will not do. Also, if you refuse to discipline little Vanessa at an early age because you lack the skill, lack the interest, cannot be bothered, or deem it too much work, then be prepared to have Vanessa by second grade refusing to cooperate and telling you and others in authority, "No, I don't want to" on a regular basis.

As you journey through this book, the idea of being flexible with your children is a tempting possibility. Flexibility is defined as, "The ability to have something modified and a willingness to compromise." On the topic of flexibility and giving chances to children after an infraction of the rules or expectations, *Be Still & Be Quiet* recommends that you adhere to structure and be consistent when dealing with young children. It is important to remember, too much flexibility and given them too many chances will result in little or no structure. Without consistency regarding rules and expectations in and outside the home, rules were made to be broken. Therefore, consistency is necessary. Teach your child to be happy and mentally healthy. Additionally, teach your child to be compassionate toward others.

You might be more flexible with adolescents and teenagers based on the situation; however, due to peer pressure and outside entities, a parental presence is essential as well in order for them to stay grounded in family values and their spirituality. A Godly home is the best home.

Even if you do everything right according to *Be Still & Be Quiet*, there is no guarantee of success. All children are born with personalities, attitudes, and free wills. Being the very best parent you can be is all that you can hope for when teaching, training, molding, role modeling, and loving God's gift to you.

Chapter 3

A Summary of Discipline

As many as I love, I rebuke and chasten: be zealous therefore, and repent

—Revelation 3:19

According to *Be Still & Be Quiet*, the key to outstanding parenting skills is good discipline. Discipline is the training you teach your child as she grows to build character, promote security, encourage appropriate behavior, and develop self-control thereby gaining an understanding of what constitutes responsible conduct and moral behavior. This is training that corrects and molds.

The difference between discipline and punishment is that punishment's purpose is to deal roughly or harshly with no teachable lesson taught or learned by the child for breaking the rules. Punishment focuses on the past. It is directed at the child in a way that will ridicule, embarrass, and/or humiliate. Punishment promotes fear, anxiety, and resentment.

Discipline on the other hand is directed at the child's behavior, not at the child. Discipline is an ongoing process of teachable moments that begins around one and certainly by age two with simple directives. Discipline provides direction and corrects behavior. Discipline is given out of love and support. It promotes a feeling of security and confidence. There will be changes to the discipline process as your child matures. Discipline continues as needed until your child leaves home.

If your child becomes a mature, well-adjusted, and healthy young adult, that means your discipline and guidance over the years have succeeded. If your child learns self-love, self-discipline, and self-determination, you have parented her well and your discipline has instilled those character traits in her that everyone can appreciate.

Discipline emphasizes all the positive self words to express emotions appropriately. It helps your child to develop self-esteem, self-control, self-reliance, self-discipline. Discipline promotes an orderly life without drama or chaos and a respect for others and their rights and property. Discipline will equip your child with an enduring character, integrity, mindfulness, kindness, the ability to resist opposition, and cope with the demands of an accelerated technological society.

A lack of discipline does not necessarily apply only to a single parent household. A passive Father or Mother in a two-parent household who wants to be a child's friend to get cooperation and love can end up with an undisciplined and out-of-control child as well.

When you, the parent, give in to inappropriate, ugly behavior, your child will repeat that behavior. There is no doubt about it. And should you become afraid of your child, she becomes the one in charge. Your child has become the parent. This is called being *parentified,* "Roles have reversed." It could be due to a fear of your child calling Child Protective Services (CPS), a fear of what people will say if you discipline your child, or a fear of your child reporting you to the police even if you spank her appropriately.

Appropriately spanking your child means not spanking her in anger. It means using a small switch on small legs if necessary to get your child to listen and pay attention to your directives which is the true purpose of spanking. Appropriate spanking is based on a child's age and size. Appropriate spanking is over with quickly and normalized through your words and actions. *Normalized* means, "The day continues with its normal routine." Hugs are given. "Love you" is expressed and all is forgiven.

To spank or not to spank is a personal choice. A spanking is effective only if it gets the desired results you want and expect. In this society, spanking or using a switch which is called a "whipping" is a no-no; but in actuality, spankings present teachable moments in which a child recognizes and learns from her mistake. She is able to openly admit her negative behavior. Utilizing a switch in your disciplinary toolbox contrasts greatly with beating a child. Punishment and beatings are designed to hurt and demean. It teaches nothing and do not demonstrate love or compassion.

When spanking or whipping their child, a parent sometimes will say, "This hurts me more than it does you." There is no doubt that most parents feel compassion and are truthful when saying this. Also, the hurt feelings and anger a spanking can cause can be lessened by a little humor or doing something so ridiculous that your child cannot help but laugh. You can do that or say something so silly that all anger dissipates. You may need to practice such humor in front of a mirror to make it work, but trust me, the payoff of you two laughing together will be worth it. The lessons your child takes away from her spanking can be many. She will be encouraged to not sweat the small stuff; this too shall pass; and do not make a mountain out of a molehill.

Such teachable moments should never happen when you have company and certainly not when you are tired, frustrated, or angry. Your toddler can sense when you want her to hurry and go to sleep because you want to get back to your visitors, friends, or family. Guess what? It is not happening. You can say, "Stop that crying and go to bed. I do not want to hear it!" a hundred times. No matter how late it is, your daughter will not go to sleep unless you and she have already resolved the issue of going to bed and right to sleep.

Your daughter knows that running away from a spanking is not an option because there are consequences. Running away demonstrates disrespect for your authority. If you are firm and consistent, your child will soon learn how not to get into trouble in the first place.

The assumption is that most parents would prefer not to spank their children but would prefer to encourage them with comments such as these:

- I love you always!
- I am impressed!
- What a great effort!
- You have the prettiest smile!
- This is a tremendous improvement!
- I never get tired of bragging about you!
- That's fabulous!
- You are so helpful!
- Thanks for helping with your baby sister!
- That's incredible!
- Fantastic!
- Excellent! That's the way to do it!
- Sensational!
- You never cease to amaze me!
- You are the best son/daughter!

The list of encouraging phrases is endless. An encouraged child is more willing to accept ideas from her parent and is not overly defensive. An encouraged child is more willing to try to please. She is able to set realistic goals; is not selfish; and, has a sense of humor.

CAUTION: Let us address a court ordered transfer of custody of a child to the grandparent or a guardian. If your grandchild or foster child is a ward of the court, spanking probably will not be an option. Children who have been spanked when their caregivers are angry can build up resentment towards them. Children going through guardianship or foster care often come with loads of inappropriate, ugly, behavior such as lying, telling half-truths, not listening, stubbornness, manipulative, and disrespectful.

A child might say, "I don't want to," "It's too hard," or "I'll do it later." That can be followed by lots of crying and stressful behavior. Please work on and demonstrate patience, patience, and more patience. You'll need it, and you'll also need to be understanding and compassionate. Be open to the possibility that mental-health counseling and medication might be necessary for such a child.

For those who believe the theory that spanking cause mental illness or harm to a child, ask yourself the following questions: When did young and middle-aged adults start killing family members? When did children start shooting classmates? When did adults start going "postal" shooting their bosses, co-workers, and complete strangers? When? Was it in the 1950's, 1960's, 1970's, 1980's, or 1990's when spanking was more acceptable?

For those opposed to spanking, ponder this: if spanking a child is so bad and some parents refuse to spank their children, why are these same parents surprised when they hear their child is not listening to the daycare provider, teachers, or anyone in authority? Why are they surprised by their child's out-of-control and bad behavior? Why are they shocked when their child curses them, hit them, run away from home, join gangs, use alcohol and drugs, or all of the above?

Should these parents be surprised by their children's disrespect for their households' family values when they, the parents, have followed the rules of society by using alternative methods of discipline such as time-outs, listening to their opinions, giving them endless chances, too many choices, and personhood?

The Family Resource Center for the prevention of child abuse offers the following age appropriate discipline techniques for two to six year olds:

- Give positive reinforcement. Focus on good behavior instead of bad behavior. Lots of praise and your full attention are the most powerful forms of positive reinforcement.
- Set an example. Redirect or show your child a better way to behave at the moment.
- Give verbal instructions. Explain what you want your child to do and why you want her to do it will help her develop good judgment.

- Give time-outs. Send your child to a neutral and boring corner of a room with no toys or TV, and ignore your child until she is calm and quiet. One minute of time-out per a child's age is a good rule of thumb. A time-out is not appropriate for a child younger than three.

Additional appropriate techniques for disciplining seven to thirteen year olds are all of the above plus the following:

- Establishing rules. Explain your rules and be prepared to repeat them as well as have your child repeat them. Having your rules posted on the refrigerator will cut down on confusion and misunderstandings. Your child needs to be told exactly what is expected just as you would teach her the rules of a new sport or game.
- Groundings. This is a consequence technique that is effective with school-age children and teenagers. Grounding involves restricting your child to a certain place, usually the home or to her room, as a consequence of an offense. Grounding will bring an overactive, overwhelmed, and stressed out child back to earth in order to relax and resolve a problem. In this case, less movement and less activity are better.
- Withholding privileges. Children should learn that privileges come with responsible behavior and are earned. To be effective, this technique should be used infrequently. Children must value their privileges such as hanging out with friends, playing on the PlayStation, talking or playing games on the phone, using the computer, going to the movie, or going to the Boys & Girls Club.

Be Still & Be Quiet recommends that parents know the correct use of praise and positive attention to reward desirable behavior. Parents usually believe they praise their children frequently. In reality, they are more likely to criticize their children for undesirable behavior than to praise them for desirable behavior. Parents need to actively praise their children for desirable behavior.

The following are suggestions on how to praise your child effectively:

- Praise the specific desirable behavior saying "Nice work" is too vague.
- Give praise as soon as possible.
- Be consistent in your use of praise.
- Avoid giving praise and criticism at the same time: "I like the way you cleaned the living room, but your room is embarrassing."
- Put some excitement in your voice to go along with the praise.

What skills do parents need to handle undesirable behavior in the home, neighborhood, supermarket, laundromat, mall, and elsewhere? How do you cope with disruptive, aggressive, and noncompliant behavior in your child? Parents should never ignore dangerous or unsafe behavior that could cause injury. A parent should try to isolate undesirable behaviors in their child such as not being quiet when directed to do so, crying excessively, throwing temper tantrums and having meltdowns, or making angry, untruthful, and hurtful statements.

Time-outs are meant to interrupt a child's undesirable behavior and to interject a consequence by depriving the child of attention through separation or isolation. A time-out should occur in a quiet room or corner and should last for only a few minutes. A time-out should be one minute for each year of a child's life up to fifteen minutes, which is about the age to replace time-outs with other age-appropriate consequences.

Time-outs should be consistent and as predictable as possible for your child. She should know where she needs to stay and how long the time-out will last. Parents should adhere to the rules.

Time-outs should end at the time agreed upon. Do not allow your child to escape from the time-out early. Do not be negligent and allow a time-out to go longer because you are on the phone, watching TV; or, are otherwise distracted.

In addition to actively ignoring negative, attention-seeking behaviors with time-outs, *Be Still & Be Quiet* offers another strategy that can prevent undesirable behavior and promote desirable behavior. It is using a behavioral chart.

A behavioral chart has a rewards component and looks like the following:

- Agree on the expected behavior, a reward for the behavior, and a consequence for misbehavior.
- Select only one behavior at a time for change.
- Discuss with the child exactly how to earn a star or a sticker on the chart.
- Involve the child in decisions about what the reward will be.
- Record successful behavior, and add up the stars or stickers.
- Give the reward at the end of the day or week.
- Be consistent in how and when you give stars or stickers.
- Give rewards and praise as a means of positive reinforcement when the child begins to be still and be quiet by no longer crying, obeying directives, or no longer breaking the rules.

Children are persistent. They can wear you down. Do not get in the habit of compromising, negotiating, making deals, or begging your child to comply with your directives. You are more effective when you are persistent and consistent. That way, you will wear her down. If you interject humor to lighten up any tension, so much the better.

Let us look at this scenario. When two year olds like, Matthew, Sabrina, Jesus, Maria, Kayla, or Joquisha do not get their way at home and have meltdowns complete with screaming, yelling, and crying, and when you are angry and frustrated, what can you do? Some parents give in to the demands of their toddler just to have peace and quiet.

However, when parents allow crying, demanding, temper tantrums to go on without correcting the negative behavior, they have in fact just begun a cycle of not challenging negativity in the future. Such behaviors might be their child not paying attention and not listening to them, being disobedient, demanding what she want and will accept nothing else, talking back, walking away from them while they are talking, and being stubborn.

If the above scenario is repeated with mother, father, family, and friends; and, if from the age of approximately two to twelve, a child learns she can get what she wants by engaging in negative, attention-seeking behavior such as excessive crying, whining, and falling out. What would be her incentive to stop? The answer of course is that there is none.

A temper tantrum that goes on for too long is a good time to call a time-out. A four year old should be in time-out for four minutes. A time-out is not to be started and restarted. If you do that, before you know it, you have continued the time-out for 15 or 20 minutes which is way too long for a four year old.

Chapter 4

How to Discipline Effectively

Mantra #1: "The more time you spend with your children when they are young, the more time they will want to spend with you when you are old"

Let us begin with Good Parenting 101. Good communication is necessary in a family. Children learn to communicate long before they speak their first words. All parents are encouraged to talk and sing to their babies while they are in the womb. Later, using their other senses, toddlers respond to ritual behavior of family members and learn to utilize verbal and nonverbal communication to get their needs met. Parents must remember the impact of their facial expressions, tones of voice, and body language when touching and holding their babies.

The way to establish good communication with your child as he matures is to encourage trust and openness. A parent cannot display wide mood swings when responding to a child's behavior good or bad. Do not be willing to listen to Muhammad and allow him to express himself one day and then the next day because of your mood refuse to listen to anything he has to say. Be consistent in your words and actions. Let your actions show you are interested in hearing your son's thoughts and dreams. That lets Muhammad know he is important to you.

Utilizing the *Be Still & Be Quiet* approach, encourage positive behavior through the following steps:

- Give your child plenty of love because he needs that. Younger children especially need lots of hugs, kisses, smiles, and praises to reassure them that they are loved. In this way, you encourage your child to repeat positive behavior. Teach your child how to be happy!
- Listen carefully to your child. If he is excited about your focus and attention, he will try harder to please you. If you work, set aside time to pay special attention and really listen to your child talk to you.
- Later, you may ask for him to focus and pay attention as you explain your excitement about an upcoming day trip to the nearest national forest, a camping trip, or a day of fishing. The time you two spend together on these outings is always time well spent as you create precious memories, bond and enjoy a healthy relationship. All adults have a need for play, relaxation, and fun time just like children.
- Your child's needs and wants change as he grows from a toddler to a teen. Listening to and observing his behavior carefully will help you prepare and deal with these changes.
- Teenagers need realistic limits when it comes to house rules and unity. Weekends might include more TV and computer time, but no cellphone calls made or received after a certain time at night. Teens are to be where they are supposed to be and obey curfews and other boundary limitations. They should be prepared for the next school day. Possibly read a book one hour before bedtime; or, read a book a week throughout the semester.
- Discuss any change in house rules, limitations, or expectations with your child. After discussing your reason for changing

your rules or establishing limits, listen to his concerns about the changes. Come to a mutual understanding, and compromise when possible.

- Be prepared for your child to test you to see if you are serious. Continue to be firm as this is a necessary process in teaching your child obedience and respect.

As a parent, it is your responsibility to teach your child in the way you would have him to grow in order to have a good and happy life. You may overlook your toddler talking back or even yelling at you, and that is okay just as long as you understand that what's cute at four years old is not cute at fourteen. If you cannot control your child, how do you expect a teacher to control him and teach at the same time? And yes, I said *control,* which has been made into a bad word though it is not. When your children become 'tweens and teenagers, you want that control to be an extension of you when you are not around.

Your children should not act like angels around you but behave devilishly or disrespectfully when you are not around! "Oh heck No." Expect and know that your children will listen to other adults and will follow rules even when you are not around. It should not be your expectation or assumption that your children will not listen to adults and will not follow the rules when you are not around. If this is your assumption, then you have nullified the core values that you have instilled in them. Also, you have underestimated your presence when you are not physically present.

Suppose your adolescent child is habitually sneaky, dishonest, a liar, and a manipulator. And suppose he does what he knows is not what he has been taught at home. I would say the guilt is the child's to own, not yours. Do not allow your child to lay a guilt trip on you. Do not accept the blame for his bad behavior. If your child says to you, "It's your fault I am this way," stay calm and reply, "The devil is a liar." Then refuse to get into a power struggle. It takes two to argue. The sin of disobedience is indeed your child's.

God has given this child to you on loan to parent. As a parent, you are commanded by God, who wants you to be an extension of Him. Indeed, you are to teach your child to obey God's Ten Commandments; to do otherwise is to not be the parent God wants you to be. You are to teach your child to know, love, and serve God. This appears to be the true purpose of life itself.

What is the age to start disciplining a child? Some would no doubt say in the womb when you sing a song or read a book to your unborn child. Some would say when your toddler knows he is making a mess for Mommy or Daddy to clean up. Also, when he is able to follow directives of, "No, do not touch." Children are innately wired to want to be cooperative and helpful. Teach your toddler early on to show empathy, concern, and thoughtfulness to others and it will carry over into his adult life.

An example would be to get your child involved in daily tasks around the house. By doing so, your child will learn that everybody works in the home together. Something to do might be washing vegetables, folding clean clothes pulled out the dryer, or putting all the toys away in the toy box. House cleaning by the whole family can be made fun with music, knock-knock jokes, funny stories, and snacks during and/or after cleaning.

Be Still & Be Quiet suggests the following aid to assist in getting young children to behave respectfully at all times. It will sustain them in all they pursue and accomplish in their lifetimes. The aid is called Stop, Look, and Listen.

- **Stop** your mannish or womanish behavior!
- **Look** at what you are doing!
- **Listen** to directives and obey!

You want to build a strong foundation of reverence in your child, again utilizing age appropriate discipline, teaching, structure, and consistency. By the time your child is 12 or 13, when most other children are misbehaving and becoming rebellious, your child will be a joy to have around due to his appropriate and respectful behavior. Good Parenting 101 is all about teaching family strength and unity.

Be Still & Be Quiet is not suggesting you deny your child's creativity and independence. In fact, discipline encourages self-esteem, confidence, independence, and creativity because nothing feels better than being at the right place and doing the right thing in harmony with your surroundings at home or in public.

Children get that concept early on if they are guided and molded in such a way that they are able to recognize fair and reasonable self-awareness and self-expression. Effective discipline helps children learn self-control, self-worth, and self-determination; in other words, all the positive self-words. Lavish praise and discipline combined will teach your child about the importance of love, family values, citizenship, character building, trust, cooperation, caring, tolerance, respect, and responsibility.

Effective methods of discipline are as follows:

- praising and rewarding positive behavior
- structuring your child's environment
- involving your child through choices and consequences
- excluding your child with a time-out
- distracting or redirecting your child into a better mood
- consistency, consistency, consistency

Here are guidelines for selecting consequences when your child is disobedient:

- Clearly express the house rules and expectations.
- The misbehavior dictates the consequence.
- Separate the deed from your child.
- Stay in the now, not with past behavior.
- Be normal, neither angry nor hostile.
- Permit choices when appropriate.

Know each child's strengths and weaknesses so that when your child, say eight or ten years old, makes a poor decision, you let the decision stand for the moment. Later, give your child another opportunity to change his attitude, choice, and cooperation. Consistently give the same consequence each time when the same misbehavior happens. Additionally, if you give your son a choice, respect your child's decision; however, you will need to make it crystal clear that there are times when he has no choice in the situation.

Let us say you decide to do nothing to interfere with or even remotely inhibit your child's independence and freedom to make his wishes known and to express himself. Suppose you say, "Discipline is not what my son needs." That is because you want him to always say what he wants, do what he wants, and have total independence even from you. Therefore, you have allowed him to make his own choices. This is called autonomy. Let us pick the ages three to twelve for this interaction.

Your child begins each day by telling you, not asking you, for things he wants because you have given him that right. Your child does not know how to say, "Please, thank you, I'm sorry, or, Mother may I?" because you have not taught him to do so. He has the choice to be good or bad, to do right or wrong. It is his choice and with choices comes power. Therefore, as the parent, you have relinquished your power to control your youngster. Your world now revolves around him and his wants. You and anyone else who comes in contact with him are at his mercy. As he matures, guess what? Independence has worked. He does not need your help in making decisions. He does not need to spend time with you as you become older because he never had to during his childhood.

Be Still & Be Quiet is talking about parents who spoil and overindulge their child with things, the latest electronic gadgetry, or electronic games. *Be Still & Be Quiet* is talking about parents who seldom make time to have dinner with their child. *Be Still & Be Quiet* is talking about parents with little or no spirituality and who seldom attend church. *Be Still & Be Quiet* is talking about parents who do not teach their children obedience from scripture and the importance of fellowship in church. *Be Still & Be Quiet* is talking about parents who

Chapter 5

Children Today

Let us say you seldom raise your voice with your child. You do favors and even inconvenience yourself for him. You have worked hard to do everything you thought was right. When you child behaves like a spoiled, unreasonable, and unappreciative child, you ask, "How is this possible? How did doing everything according to the professionals cause me to have an undisciplined and disrespectful child?"

I am glad you asked. It is because you have catered to him over the years, looked the other way when you should not have, begged and pleaded with him to behave, given autonomy to him, and tried not to be too hard on him. So why is he disrespectful and acting out with feelings of entitlement from everyone he meets?

When you take your undisciplined and inattentive child for his first day of preschool, remember that this is the same child who just the previous week had refused to allow you to hold his hand to cross the street without creating a scene. This is the same child who will not pay attention to most if not all of your directives. The question to ask is, "Why should my child behave appropriately at school if I have not given him the training and skills at home to be still, be quiet, and pay attention during the first five years of his life?"

Now, for some reason, you expect your child to obey and respect a complete stranger, his teacher. You also now expect his teacher to do what you were unable to do during your child's first five years. Your child starts preschool without having learned discipline. He is unable or unwilling to listen to directives and frequently displays out-of-control behavior.

Again, if for whatever reason you have not disciplined your child that is a problem. One solution is that the school might need for the safety of all, teacher, your child, and other children to have your child tested for (ADD), attention deficit disorder, or (ADHD), attention deficit hyperactivity disorder. Children with short attention spans and a difficult time concentrating are generally diagnosed as having ADD. ADHD has added hyperactivity or "bouncing off the wall" behavior. Once tested by a professional and if diagnosed with one of these disorders, counseling and possibly medication might be needed.

A first grade teacher cannot teach a class with an out-of-control child. Perhaps your child is unstructured, disobedient, rude, disrespectful, loud, and disruptive, does not listen to adults, and does not follow the rules. If so, your child is on a collision course with society as a whole and the rules of the land. Having poor or no social skills leads to a child making errors in judgment outside normal and acceptable behavior. To miscue on what is appropriate and fair will keep a child on the outside looking in and on the road to becoming a misfit.

Entitlement and breaking the rules of society can get an adolescent into a lot of trouble especially with law enforcement. Juvenile delinquents break the law, fight at school, ditch school, vandalize property, shop-lift, and more. If your son is ever arrested, he will become involved with the juvenile justice legal system. He might be cited out with a court date in a month or two; or he could be held at a juvenile facility until his court appearance. Usually, after a couple of court appearances, a decision is made as to whether your child is to be sentenced, discharged from custody, or placed on probation for a year. Another scenario would be that your child is placed on an electronic ankle monitor (EM).

In bewilderment, you ask, "Why has my child chosen to break

the law, get arrested, and be placed in a locked facility called juvenile hall?" A juvenile delinquent can be any out-of-control child. Often, out-of-control children are diagnosed with oppositional-defiant disorder. If your child's behavior has deteriorated and offenses against the home or society are worse due to a complete disregard for others, counseling by a mental health professional might be needed.

The delinquent's behavior is in sharp contrast to a child who behaves with respect, pride, compassion, high self-esteem, and self-control. Self-control is a personal decision by a child and must be decided with insight and foresight.

Today's parents are often afraid of their child. Their fear can stem from excessive permissiveness as well as little or no structure or discipline in the home. The child lives a life of complete chaos and does as he pleases with no orderliness or consequences. Some parents hide their fear of raising their children by trying to be their child's BFF (best friend forever). A disobedient, spoiled, rude, and disrespectful child comes to no good end.

How many times have you heard or know of parents who allows their child, whether a teenager or young adult, to call them by their first names? The children in the home are allowed to talk to their parents as if they are on the same level or equals. To treat a child as an equal is ridiculous. To allow a child to call you by your first name is so disrespectful because your role as parent is for a lifetime; and, he is your child, later on he is your adult child, for life.

If your child asks, "When can I call you by your first name?" The answer is, "Never." Your teenager or young adult might occasionally joke with you by calling you by your first name. If you have such a relationship, this is fine. However, the boundaries of your parenting role should always be clear. Do not muddy the water with unclear or ever-changing boundaries and role reversals. If a child does not demonstrate respect for his parent, why would he show respect to a stranger, an elder, or an authority figure? A child who barks out orders to his parents and tells them, not asks them, to do this or that is definitely in the parenting business. Make no mistake about it, the parenting roles have been reversed.

Many of today's children have lost their way. They have learned to manipulate and control their parents, grandparents, and relatives by lying, talking back, yelling, cussing, arguing, intimidating, assaulting them, or running away. Out-of-control children are not going to school. They are not prideful of their schools, disrespect their schools, are not trying to get an education, are parenting themselves; and, are not taking responsibility for their negative behavior.

Where were the parents who saw the beginnings of these outrageous behaviors and negative influences but did nothing to guide their child back to good virtues and moral living? Parents who turn a blind eye to their preteens' and teenager' disrespectful attitude. Who let their child hang out with troublesome crowds, put up with his talking back, not listening, cursing, dressing inappropriately, ditching classes, and failing or refusing to complete chores and schoolwork have only themselves to blame.

Unless some serious intervention occurs immediately such as consequences for bad behavior, improved supervision, and possibly counseling to instruct and direct changes in your child's thinking and behavior, he could have ongoing violations of probation and become a repeat juvenile offender. Alcohol and drug used by 11 year olds is not uncommon in an undisciplined, unstructured, and promiscuous household. A child joining a gang, doing work to stay in the gang, being a backup for a gang, sporting tattoos, and running away is common.

The phrase "Today's children do things differently" is often an excuse some parents use to do nothing to discipline or even aid their children. It is an excuse for some parents to avoid assisting their children with projects, monitoring their homework, or helping them prepare for school tests and quizzes.

The sad truth of the matter is that some children, especially those in grade school, are identified at a young age as high risk for dropping out of school. Some third graders will be labeled as troublesome, ill-prepared, and without structure based on observable family dynamics.

Your son needs his Father's guidance because freedom to make his own choices comes with taking responsibility for those choices. By educating your son, you will reveal to him the limits of freedom in order to live in harmony with others.

The quality time you spend together is good for your relationship because you will learn his interests, strengths, hobbies, and ambitions in early preparation for the rest of his life.

Your child will usually get four nights of homework per week, none on Friday. Parents should set aside time for homework before children are allowed to talk on the phone, play, or hang out with friends. Doing homework should be non-negotiable. It needs to happen! As your child matures, he will one day thank you for providing the guidance he needed to develop good study habits that easily led to good work habits. He may not thank you in words. It might be in how he excels in high school.

The two questions that beg to be asked are, "Who is in charge?" and "What is your role as a parent?" Parents are in charge and their role is to train their children to be respectful of their elders, proud of their accomplishments, love their parents, their communities, their schools, and to honor those in authority. This happens when they grow up in loving, but structured home, with fair and consistent rules.

If you are a parent, then parent, because a child expects no less. If you do a good job as a parent and take care of the life God has entrusted you with, you will reap the benefits of what you sow. All the hard work of instilling God's spirituality. His love, your love, structure, consistency, and discipline in the home will come back to you in the form of a healthy, well-adjusted, courageous, empathetic, and self-disciplined child you will be proud of for a lifetime.

Chapter 6

Tiger Mom

A tiger Mom is a label given to Mothers and Fathers who stereotypically raise successful children by being strict parents who focus exclusively on their children's academic perfection. These parents hope to produce children who are able to achieve academic excellence, musical mastery, and professional success.

Amy Chua wrote "Why Chinese Mothers Are Superior" in the *Wall Street Journal* on January 8, 2011. It generated much global debate on what constitutes good parenting. In the essay, Chua listed some of the things she never allowed her children to do:

- attend a sleepover
- have a play date
- be in a school play
- watch TV/play computer games
- choose their own activities
- get any grade less than an A
- not be the top student in every subject except gym and drama
- play any instrument other than the piano or violin

This is Chua's list. Most Americanized families would have a difficult time utilizing this list in parenting their children.

The hope of any good parenting technique or style is for your child to master education, which is critical when it comes to a successful career and a wonderful life. A city bus in Fresno, California, once displayed a sign that read, "Anywhere you want to go, education will take you there." No truer words were ever written. And ponder this, Dr. Jawanza Kunjufu has said many times, "It's easier to educate than to incarcerate."

Be Still & Be Quiet wants you to know that the motivating factor for success is extensive preparation. Parents, spend time with your child. Teach your child good work ethics. Instruct her on how to work smart and hard for what she wants to accomplish and to never quit. The spiritual guidance and family values learned as a child will stay with her for the rest of her life.

Chapter 7

No Structure, No Routine, No Nap

Suppose you have chosen to be a stay-at-home Mom. Without structure or routine, your child is constantly on the move with you. If you do not give her a daily nap, she is never still or quiet until sleep is so overpowering that she cannot fight it anymore. That usually occurs when you are driving. She will drop off to sleep in the car seat traveling from Walmart to the dry cleaners because that is the only time she has been given to take a nap.

After this mini nap, she feels a burst of energy and is ready to go again until she can no longer hold up her head and sleep is calling her name. It is not the child's fault that she is on an adult's schedule without a specific time for naps and bedtime.

Without a regular babysitter or some form of respite care, your child will likely be with adults more than children. Her schedule will be a grown-up schedule that can go into the night well after 10:00 or 11:00 before the child is put to bed for the night. Then the real battle begins with your toddler telling you, "I don't wanna go to bed!" This she says over and over. This battle can last 30 minutes to over an hour.

As the parent, you are not listening but instead getting angry because in all probability you are also tired. So with tears streaming down your toddler's cheeks, we have a classic meltdown due to extreme tiredness by all living in the household. No, your child is not "acting" or being a "drama queen." After all, who would have given her drama lessons if not you? But, in all likelihood, your child has learned that she can get what she wants through negative attention seeking crying behavior. Now, you feel like spanking your daughter out of anger because you are tired, sleepy, and want to go to bed. It is apparent that you usually discipline when angry without purpose other than to lash out at your child in frustration. When it comes to healthy practices, your child needs structure, a routine, and a daily nap.

Once the house is quiet, unless the Mother or Father has to go to work, everyone in the house will probably sleep late. The next morning, your child is on the move with you to do it all over again. Even if you are not a stay-at-home Mom or Dad, if your child is running her own program, when you come home from work, most of the evening is spent yelling at your toddler who has selective hearing. Could this be the same child that you unintentionally taught to yell and scream when she wants something?

Another possibility is that your child is getting mixed messages regarding discipline from you, the daycare provider, and the babysitter. Are there house rules and structure in place for the babysitter until you come home from work; or, are there no rules and no discipline? If nothing is in place, no wonder your child is confused.

As the parent, you should know if your child's care provider is easygoing with few rules; or, if the provider is firm and disciplined in their style of providing care. Consistency matters. Sending mixed messages to a child is confusing and encourages oppositional-defiant behavior.

A child quickly figures out who the players are and what their expectations are during a typical day. Therefore, do not wonder why she is crying, being rebellious, hardheaded and difficult, acting out, or just plain misbehaving. How you care for your child also affects society. It is not okay for you to practice poor parenting and poor health care for your child whether it is her eating or sleeping habits because ultimately, society will have to pay the price for your child's angry, loud, disrespectful, manipulative, and out-of-control behavior.

A child cannot spend the first five years of her life constantly talking and walking nonstop until she drops off to sleep. When a child gets the proper amount of sleep, which includes daily naps and early to bed, it allows her mind and body to relax and rejuvenate.

Children from one to seven need at least 11 to 13 hours of sleep a day. They also need mid-day naps to recharge their bodies and minds. Those eight to fourteen years old need at least 8 to 10 hours of sleep. Older teenagers need at least 8 hours of sleep a night, especially on school nights.

Even with daily structure and a nap routine, there are times when you need to have things for your daughter to do and play with such as her favorite toy, a coloring book, or a snack.

Chapter 8

Tips to End Bedtime Drama

Examples of negative behavior by a three year old at bedtime could be the following:

- Your child is sitting on the bed and saying over and over, "I don't want to go to bed!"
- Your child is making a crying sound without tears.
- Your child is angry and throwing toys everywhere.
- Your child is having a temper tantrum, kicking, screaming, and rolling around on the floor.
- Your child will not be quiet no matter how many times you plead with him.

You will need to establish a consistent course of action to get the obedience and good behavior you are looking for in your child. Be specific when telling your child what you want him to do, which in this case is go quietly to bed. Instead, your toddler is crying and saying, "I don't want to go to bed!"

As a good parent, you put your child to bed with the night light on and inform your son of your expectations. If he stops crying, the light stays on. If not, it goes off. It is hard to turn the light off if the crying does not stop. You might have to turn it off and on several times before your child stops crying. This may be necessary if you want to teach your child the particular behavior you want. You might have to repeat this bedtime practice for weeks with consistency before the bedtime drama stops but it will stop. Once your child has stopped crying and is cooperating by lying down, you immediately give him praise, kisses, and hugs.

When children are between three and about eight, read to them at bedtime. When they are old enough to read, they can read to you at their bedtime.

Parents need to know and understand that their children are not miniature adults. They have neither the experience nor the maturity to make the right decisions. They are not three year olds going on six or eight. They might say some mature things; or, act older than their age, but the fact is they are merely mimicking what they see and hear. The age appropriate decision making is not there yet.

CAUTION: If, however, innocence is stolen from a young child who sees and is shown how to do inappropriate things, then talking mature and acting grown for that child is a different story with obvious red flags. It is a horrific story that could, if not already reported, requires reporting, possibly resulting in a criminal investigation and mental health counseling.

As a parent, you must take the time to get past the crying, the demanding, or the power struggles your child engage you in because he does not know what he needs. Even if a child appears to know what he wants, who is the parent and who is the child?

When a child has learned that you hate to tell him no, it is a sad time because power struggles will be inevitable. When a child knows that if he asks you more than three or four times to do something, he will get what he wants. That is scary! If a child has learned that if he asks a little later or after you have had a few drinks to help you relax, he will get what he wants. That is terrifying! If a child knows he has won the battle for control whether he is five or sixteen, you, the parent, are in trouble. No should mean no, not maybe, and definitely not, "Ask me again in a little while."

To be a good parent, grandparent, adoptive parent, or guardian, you must teach your child that you cannot be manipulated, which is a learned behavior, but it can be unlearned. Therefore, refuse your child when you must so he will not learn to manipulate, use and abuse others when he is older. You want your child to learn to love people and use things. The opposite of that would be for your child to learn to love things and use people.

Chapter 9

An Action Plan

Be Still & Be Quiet would like to introduce an action plan for effective parenting skills designed to prevent negative oppositional-defiant behavior by your child that causes heartbreak to you, a grandparent, foster parent, or adoptive parent.

If, when you read *Be Still & Be Quiet*, your child is older but still having behavioral and school problems, there are tips for improved behavior of your tween and teenager in other sections of this book.

With *Be Still & Be Quiet*'s action plan, you will take control of your two to five year old misbehaving by giving her a specific time-out called, "Let's Do Better." It comes from the saying, "When you know better, do better." You will need to demonstrate for your toddler by sitting still and quiet on the couch beside her for five or ten minutes as you role play the behavior you want. This then is a teachable moment. At the end of a proper time-out, your little angel will likely have forgotten what she had been fussing and crying about.

While sitting on the couch with your toddler, the "Let's Do Better" time-out does not mean your child is asking for water every second or getting up to get a toy. You will need to *Be Still & Be Quiet* as well during this training. It does not mean Mom or Dad is engrossed in conversation with someone in the room or on your phone. *Still* means without movement, and *Quiet* means without sound. *Be Still*

& Be Quiet does not mean your child is talking nonstop, singing, wiggling around, or retrieving this or that from all over the house.

Be Still & Be Quiet does not recommend giving a treat after a time-out. Discipline by a time-out is to be normalized and treated as part of the day's routine. When a child is having a meltdown, she can be given a time-out. Again, the behavior does not include a reward for disobedience. To give a reward in such a case is to teach your child in that teachable moment how to be manipulative. When a reward is withheld, your child learns that to be good is expected and is not out of the ordinary. Your child learns that obedience is a reward in itself. This strengthens the relationships between the child and the parent and other care providers.

As your child matures, understands and agrees to obey limits, she is also learning to set her own limits, which promotes independence. You will provide encouragement, comfort, and support when your child experiences success as well as failure. Failure should be treated as a learning experience. The saying goes, "You fall down. You get up and brush yourself off. Tomorrow is another day."

Be Still & Be Quiet believes that every day should be a day for learning something new and different. Why? I'm glad you asked! Because today is a day that you have never seen before; and, it is a day that you will never see again. Your daughter should be encouraged to like to learn and then practice, practice, what was learned, then practice some more.

Whether your daughter is experiencing success or failure, she will need your support to feel happy about taking risks and developing the perseverance needed to get the task done. Give your child daily chores as her contribution to the home. This will promote an understanding of hard work, organization, accepting responsibility, and self-confidence. If an eight or nine year old has a good reason for not getting chores done, set a time limit for when the chore must be completed. Physically check to make sure the chore is completed in a timely fashion. Praise your child for completing it. This will help her develop confidence in self.

Within a few weeks or a few months of implementing *Be Still &
Be Quiet's* Action Plan for unruly behavior and breaking house rules, a
parent should see improved attitude and purpose. At no time should a
time-out be used for extended periods of time as a punishment. *Be Still
& Be Quiet* is simply for discipline and getting your child's attention
for a specific misdeed. It is not to ever become child abuse; such as,
time-out for hours or most of the day, depriving a child from using
the bathroom, or, going to sleep. Time-outs should be tied to a child's
age, a three year old should go in time-out for three minutes and a five
year old for no longer than five minutes. You consistently discipline
unruly behavior or breaking a rule with love, not anger.

What if a young child refuses to be still and be quiet in her quest
to exert power? Power struggles and a battle of wills occur when a
child thinks she is in charge. If she is angry, falling out on the floor,
and having a real meltdown, you will need to have her sit on your
lap with you holding her in a gentle bear hug until she calms down.
Your child might cry for 20 or 30 minutes, but she will get tired, calm
down, and go to sleep. Over the next few weeks with consistency, all
you will need to say is "Come, get on my lap." Your child should then
be willing to get on your lap and calm down due to a normalized and
predictable routine to achieve peace.

Parents cannot teach discipline and obedience effectively unless
they are consistent. You cannot practice *Be Still & Be Quiet* today
and allow disruptive or negative behavior the next day; or, after a 3rd
or 4th time, decide it is too much work; or, you do not have the time
to be bothered. If you are consistent, you will teach your child that
you expect positive behavior. Negative behavior is nipped in the bud
before it can take root.

With consistency, your child will eventually learn to put herself
in quiet time by playing quietly with a toy, using her imagination to
be creative, and being quiet without being told. Your child will learn
how to wait for things she wants and how to earn them by behaving
appropriately. She will not expect instant gratification. She will know,
who is the parent and who is the child?

Your child will have respect for you, the Mother, and you, the Father. She will no longer challenge you. She will trust that you know what is best for her. By being a parent who is firm, consistent rather than inconsistent; and, who does not give mixed messages, you are preparing your child for the world. You are teaching skills that will be needed in preschool, kindergarten, high school, college, adulthood, the work force, and throughout life.

Utilizing the *Be Still & Be Quiet* approach:

1. For your younger child, a sharp "No" or a "Stop it" should be effective in stopping unnecessary, crying, behavior. However, if you scold or yell too often and for too long without any consequences, your child might stop listening to you.
2. Time-out will give your child age three and older a chance to cool off and stabilize. Take a time-out for yourself if needed.
3. Avoid sending your child to his room. Instead, choose a corner of the house, like the kitchen or living room, as a calming spot.
4. Tell your child how long he will be in time-out.
5. Make it clear to your child that the time-out will start over if he comes out of the designated spot which is preferably a room you are in.
6. Make sure your child is in a safe place physically, mentally, and emotionally. If your child is too upset, wait until he has calmed down.
7. As the time-out comes to an end, discuss with your child what just happened.
8. Spank your child as a last resort. *Be Still & Be Quiet* does not want physical discipline to become your first response to negative behavior.
9. As your son becomes older, remove privileges for disobedience and disrespect. This can include turning off the computer, video game, cellphone, tablet, iPhone, iPod, TVs.

10. Suppose you have no cable TV. Then you might have a smart TV and do a lot of streaming on Netflix, Hula, Roku, or Amazon prime. This will also become the takeaway if your son misbehaves. Netflix comes with a parental control application (app) that works with small and older children. Take away from your child what he likes best. You might need to add Snapchat, Instagram, Twitter, and all internet access.

11. Should your adolescent damage or destroy property, if possible, have him fix it or pay for it out of his allowance. Your child will admit wrongdoings and apologize to the owner of the property. By your son admitting to doing something wrong and saying he is sorry, a valuable lesson has been learned. The lesson is, we try to make a wrong, right again! Normalize an "I'm sorry" because it is the gentleman thing to do.

12. Wrongdoing is not to be negotiated, compromised, sidestepped, minimized, or excused, and its consequences are not to be put off until tomorrow if it can be dealt with today.

Here are other guidelines when your child misbehaves include the following:

13. Be prompt with discipline so your child associates misbehavior with the consequences.

14. Make sure your child understands why you are disciplining him.

15. Set a time-out limit and tell your child how long his consequences will last. A time-out should last a short time whereas privileges can be lost for several days.

16. Control your emotions. Do not discipline when you are angry or emotional.

17. Tell your child that because of your love for him, you must enforce house rules and directives.

18. Avoid empty threats or nagging because your child will stop paying attention or will respect you less because you do not follow through with what you said you would do.

19. Consequences should always fit the inappropriate, acting-out, behavior.
20. Whatever happened to writing 100 or 200 sentences of "I will do" or "I will not do" such and such?
21. Good old-fashioned grounding still works to keep your child close to home due to bad behavior elsewhere. This is a loss of privilege.
22. Loss of privilege for failed grades. This means no outside play, possibly no school activities, and certainly no social events. All fun is halted until grades have improved.
23. When possible, scold in private, not in front of your child's friends.
24. Involve your child in finding a solution for his bad behavior.

If you shield or overly protect your child from the consequences of his behavior, you are preventing him from learning from his mistake, taking responsibility for his action, and maturing emotionally and spiritually, all happening at the same time. The balance here is to spend quality time with your child to ensure a good relationship with him. It is a relationship intended to prevent your child from developing behavioral problems, bad attitudes, negative friendships, and becoming a follower later on. Always remember that sarcasm, ridicule, and unnecessary pressure are destructive to a close and loving relationship.

Chapter 10

Role Modeling

Be the person you want your child to become. Be a living, day-to-day example of your values, attitudes, integrity, thoughtfulness, kindness, and willingness to help others. Show the compassion, honesty, generosity, gentleness, and openness you want your child to have.

Model the behavior you want to see in your child. If you want her to be trustworthy, tell the truth. Your child learns from watching you. If you want her to be on time, you must be punctual yourself. If you want your child to pick up after herself, pick up after yourself. If you want your child to turn down the volume and not be loud then you must speak in a moderate to soft voice, model that behavior. If you want your child to be polite, you must set an example by saying, "Please," "Sorry," and "Thank you" when talking to others.

Do not allow your child to bark out orders and make demands of you or any adult. Teach your child to use the magic word *please* when she asks for something. Whether it is a grandMother, guardian, aunt, cousin, neighbor, teacher, or law enforcement, they all deserve respect from your child. Teach her to address her elders as Sir, Ma'am, Big Mama, Nana, Grandpa Juan, Miss Julia Mae, Aunt Christine, Uncle Earl, Cousin Bennie, and so on. Family and neighbors do not have to be elderly to get this respectful greeting. Your child should be taught that good manners apply to all adults but especially to the elderly. It should be explained to them that older adults have interesting life stories to tell them if they are quiet, attentive, and have good listening skills

Do not allow your child to stare you down and refuse to move when given a directive. Never tolerate a battle of wills to see who blinks first, you or your child. There must be consequences for defiance and a bad attitude for any child living at home.

Teach your children good communication skills. They should learn not to answer you with, "What?" or "Huh?" They should learn to say, "Yes sir," "Yes ma'am" or "Sorry, I didn't hear you."

Some will say children's response today is abrupt, loud, and aggressive; however, demonstrating manners is how they should respond if they have a proper upbringing.

In another generation, the belief was, "A child should be seen and not heard." This holds true even to this day. When adults discuss grown-up affairs or business, children should be excused from the room and remain out until invite back into the room. Children will sometimes attempt to eavesdrop by standing near adults, pretending to be doing something. If the topic being discussed is too mature in nature and is none of their business or concern, your child leaving the room should not be up for discussion or argument. Your child can do only what you allow her to do. Children who are taught to stay in their place do not question or challenge their parents' beliefs or values. A child need not know what adults know and when they knew it.

Chapter 11

Religion

He that spareth his rod hateth his son; but, he that loveth him chasteneth him betimes.

—Proverbs 13:24

With this biblical quote, what are we talking about? We are talking about spankings designed to get your child's attention. You are the parent and therefore the disciplinarian. A spanking should be your last resort.

The use of the switch is for an older child who knowingly, stubbornly, and angrily challenges you. Use a switch on a child only after he repeatedly refuses to listen to you after having been warned several times that there will be consequences for misbehaving. Maybe raising your voice will be all you need to do, but usually, raising your voice doesn't work if that is all you are prepared to do.

Whatever works for you and your child, be consistent. Inconsistent, straddling the fence, or wishy-washy will only lead to your child manipulating you and showing total disregard for what you say or do. Manipulation can be in the form of anger, the silent treatment, and selective hearing until you give into his demand.

When talking about spanking or using a switch, we are not talking about beating or abusing your child with an extension cord, a shoe, or a stick. For some parents, the mention of corporal punishment makes the hair on the back of their necks stand up. They visualize extreme cases of punishment, beatings, even slavery. But *Be Still & Be Quiet* is always about exercising restraint, remaining calm, and displaying patience when disciplining.

If harsh, unfair, and loveless discipline is the only interaction between you and your child, it is a form of abuse that can provoke your child to anger, rebellion, defiance, and resentment. Abuse of parental power also leads youngsters or teenagers to becoming defiant and not listening to you or other adults in authority. Too often, this leads to teenagers and young adults who will not obey any rules. They are often disrespectful, curse parents and teachers, are disruptive in class, receive multiple suspensions and expulsions from school. They are oppositional and defiant, argue, fight, and run away from home. It is your choice how you discipline or choose not to discipline.

> *Many will see, and fear, and put their trust in the Lord.*
> —Psalm 40:3

Some people believe that if your child is afraid of you, he will not respect you. This is an untruth. Children who fear Father God, parents, grandparents, adopted parents, guardians, teachers, law enforcement personnel, and others in authority are more likely to have a positive attitude, high self-esteem, and pride in self, home, and school. They experience numerous successes in the home and when interacting with peers and society as a whole.

Your child will respect you when he realizes you love him and want only the best for him. A lifetime of hugs, kisses, and terms of endearment will guarantee a closeness between you and your child that will never change.

Be Still & Be Quiet is about disciplining your son or daughter from toddler to teenager. Your action plan should include being firm, nurturing, spending time with your child, talking with your child, and really listening to him when he is talking to you while still disciplining him when necessary.

Indeed, by the age of 10 or 12, your child should be more than willing to listen to you, be respectful, and obey you. Out of love and respect, he should not want to upset or disappoint you. Your display of hugs and love toward him should nullify any negative reaction from past spankings or other means of discipline. As a teenager, oppositional-defiant behavior should be rare.

Mantra # 2: A family that prays and plays together stays together

This mantra is effective in most households. It is suggested that you put it in a prominent place such as on your refrigerator and recite it every day much like an affirmation. If this is your mantra, your child will walk by faith and not by sight in his obedience to God and to you.

> *And all thy children shall be taught of the Lord, and great shall be the peace of thy children.*
>
> —Isaiah 54:13

Priests with children

Be Still & Be Quiet emphasizes teaching your child prayer, forgiveness, love, cooperation, and sharing. A Mother declares, "Devil, take your hands off my child." She then makes is happen by serving Father God and teaching her child to love and obey God's Ten Commandments. Be the teacher and teach your child that the Lord's house is not the place for him to play games on his tablet or smartphone. If two children are next to each other, they will talk and play as if they were outside and not in the Lord's house. The question to ask is, "Why does your child have this distraction in the first place?" At best, give him a pencil and paper and let him draw. That should be sufficient. There is no better place to teach your child to be still and be quiet than in God's house!

Be still and know that I Am God.

—Psalm 46:10

Chapter 12

Get Your Mind Straight
and Your Body Right

Parents, listen up! Would you please dress appropriately in the Lord's house? Leave your jeans at home. This admonition applies especially to women. When you come to God's house, be respectful. Contrary to some people's belief, what you wear matters. *Be Still & Be Quiet* takes the position that if you dress down, your faith will appear to be down in the dumps in mind and spirit as well. If you dress up in your Sunday best for church, you send a message about your state of mind. Ask yourself, "Why do I dress up for social events or a nice restaurant but not for God? What's wrong with this picture?"

If parents can dress appropriately for work or a job interview, that same Mother or Father should be able to dress up on Saturday or Sunday morning for the Lord to go to His house? Why wear inappropriate jeans? A Mother would not wear a midrib halter-top to church, would she? As a Father, you would not go to church shirtless, would you?

It is unimaginable that someone would doubt that the church represents God's house. Your child will dress in jeans for church if she sees you dress in jeans for church. She will copy your point of view and your attitude about what to wear and how to present herself to the world when attending church. Your child should have three sets of clothes to change into. She should have church clothes, school clothes, and play clothes.

When you mentally and spiritually prepare yourself for church by reading your Holy Bible, you might want to cut off worldly, loud, and distracting music 30 minutes prior to starting out the door for church. You are getting your mind right.

Next, get your body right with the proper attire. If you are so poor that you need to save your best clothes for job interviews, wearing jeans to church is understandable. If you wear jeans only because your church is not a fashion show, you are right! However, every time you step outside your front door, the world becomes a stage. The public and social media are watching how you present yourself.

If you are traveling out of town on vacation and all you have in your suitcase is jeans and casual wear, possibly you forgot to bring clothes for church, wearing jeans is excusable.

Other excuses for possibly wearing jeans to church are: too lazy to prepare your clothes the night before; bored with the task of going to church weekly; becoming too complacent; a lukewarm Christian; and/or having feelings of entitlement in the House of the Lord.

As parents, you must always be a role model for your children who look up to you. They mimic what they see you do. Please get your mind straight and your body right.

Chapter 13

A Hug a Day

All parents want their children to have a good attitude when asked to do something. When your son, Adam, has a positive and righteous attitude, be quick to give him a hug. Also, let Adam know that you love him no matter what situation just occurred. Do not give hugs for a bad attitude. Oppositional-defiant behavior comes with consequences. Chores will still have to be done and privileges may be lost.

You want cooperation, not opposition. You want a team player. You want sharing, caring, and participation. When you get this exceptional behavior from your son, give him a big hug. Daily hugs result in less defiance and resentment from Adam when it comes to house rules, directives, or requests.

Mantra #3: A hug a day keeps defiance away

Even if children and adolescents display the best and healthiest behavior at home, at church, and at public events, they can sometime lapse into "off the chart" behavior due to the desire to fit in with peers by acting out, primarily in school. The desire is to "get in where you fit in." With the proper foundation, this should be a temporary setback because Adam will have skills learned a long time ago about appropriate self-expression, self-awareness, and self-control, the three selves. He will have learned to regulate his behavior, which means to calm down and become less amped up and hyperactive. In other words, your child knows how to *Be Still & Be Quiet*.

If your son exhibits healthy behavior and a good attitude with no complaints, give him rewards, incentives, enticements, and encouragement to keep that up. Incentives for small children could be trips to the zoo, walks in the park, or playing in the playground.

An incentive for a 12, 13, or 14 year old might be getting into sports. It can be very expensive and require financial help from Mom and Dad, as well as, transportation to and from practices and games. Your adolescent should be rewarded for improved grades from last semester. Adam should receive an allowance for assisting an elderly relative or neighbor. Other chores for an allowance might be learning to play a musical instrument, taking a singing or dancing class, swim or tennis lessons and playing in tournaments, washing windows, cleaning the entire bathroom (sink, toilet, mirror, bath tub, and floor). Can you think of anything else in the bathroom? Just joking! Allowances should come for doing daily or weekly household chores, working on the family car with Dad, cutting and styling hair, and learning how to repair bicycles and small appliances. You will want to include appropriate activities that appeal to and motivate him to be productive.

Your teenager might secure an internship at a construction site, learn from a plumber, research a topic, build something, work on a trade, or develop a skill. Other rewards for positive behavior might be joining Pop Warner, Cub Scouts, Brownies, Boys and Girls Clubs, Big Sisters & Big Brothers, and the Police Activities League (PAL).

Rewards are getting a prize, a trophy, a payment, a promise, going to an event, or receiving a gift. Other examples of tasks that reap rewards are completing chores without complaining, cleaning up after a pet, clean the garage, or reading a book. Additional rewards might be a trip to the ice cream parlor, arcades, going to a movie, roller-skating, allowing a sleepover at a friend's house, or getting a cellphone back.

Examples of takeaways might include denying a sleepover at a friend's home, being grounded for the day, or no cellphone for neglecting to call home as directed.

If what you are doing as a parent is still not working and you are at your wit's end, professional help might be needed in the form of counseling, medication, or both. Getting a referral from your child's pediatrician for a psychiatric evaluation could be your next step. This often results in a mental health diagnosis followed by individual and family counseling.

Fun Family Activities

Several fun activities are listed below. Fun activities are intended to keep parent and child connected in a trusting and loving relationship.

Ages 3 to 6
1. Daycare at church
2. Watering flowers
3. Playing in a sandbox
4. Raking leaves for play
5. Coloring book/activities
6. Go to playground
7. Swim in a kiddie pool
8. Birthday parties
9. Feed ducks in a pond
10. Taking walks
11. Learning the ABCs
12. Learning numbers
13. Going to a pumpkin patch

Ages 7 to 13
1. Going to church/reading scriptures
2. Movies/theater
3. Playing video games
4. Family bicycle riding to the park
5. Rollerblading/skateboarding
6. Shopping at a grocery store
7. Cook breakfast
8. Planning a birthday party
9. Go to the circus
10. Family picnics
11. Helping grandma
12. Helping with homework
13. Free events at the library

14. A trip to the zoo
15. Riding bike/training wheels
16. Singing/dancing

17. Walking the dog

18. Family picnics

19. Telling knock- knock jokes

20. Gardening
21. Taking a nap

22. Eating dinner together

14. Going trick or treating
15. Zoo outing
16. Going to the Boys/Girls Club
17. Join Cub Scouts/Brownies of America
18. Take meditation and/or Tai Chi classes
19. Telling clean and appropriate jokes
20. Dancing/singing
21. Take up a new hobby/ interests
22. Participating in sports
23. Talking long distance
24. FaceTime, Skype, video messaging
25. Watch a favorite TV show
26. Solve a problem/puzzle
27. Play chess/cards/dominoes
28. Care for a pet
29. Write letters to friends/ relatives
30. Eat dinner together

Chapter 14

The Public Arena

When you and your toddler step outside the house, you enter the public arena whether you are going to the grocery store, visiting friends and relatives, or going to the laundromat. Be careful about disciplining your child in public. Your child will have an audience; so, you will not have her full attention for a teachable moment. Additionally, people will be quick to think the worst and get involved in how you should or should not discipline your child. Public concern is understandable during an act of discipline due to the fear of possible child abuse in public and/or in the privacy of your home.

Children are wonderful but they are not the center of others' universes. People do not love your five or six year old when you allow her to yell, scream, and run rampant in restaurants, department stores, the doctor's office, or the bank.

Parents will not do their children any favors by spoiling them, indulging their every demand, allowing a sense of entitlement, encouraging instant gratification, or allowing out-of-control and disruptive behavior.

How many times have you seen a Mother, it is usually not the Father, in public trying to get control of her child who is not listening, running wild, and yelling in total disregard for what the Mother is telling her? The Mother says, "Get over here now! Stop that and come here like I told you. Why aren't you listening to me?"

Does that sound familiar? Sometimes, the child does as directed, but shortly thereafter, she is again not listening and doing as she pleases. Who is the parent and who is the child? This is an undisciplined three to six year old who has too much freedom and gets too many choices. The Mother should direct the child, not the other way around.

"Adaku baby, do you want to go to grandmother's house; or, do you want to stay here and play at McDonald's?" Say what? Why is this youngster deciding anything; whether it is what she wants to eat, to wear, when to leave, or to go to sleep? Who is the parent?

If this were a *Be Still & Be Quiet* teachable moment, the Mother would simply say, "Give me your hand" and the child would do so without argument or debate. Adaku would not ask questions and expect answers to them. If she asked, "Why do I have to hold your hand?" the Mother would say, "Because I said so," end of story, no guilt trip, no explanation. Peace and cooperation can happen if taught with love, consistency, patience, and consequences.

Out in public, in a *Be Still & Be Quiet* teachable moment, it might be the right time to teach Adaku that when you are talking to another adult, she is to say, "Excuse me" and wait for a response.

Imagine this scene, hopefully you can avoid it

Child: "Mommy, Mommy! I want ice cream."
Mother: "Wait just one minute, honey, Mommy's talking."
Child: "Mommy, Mommy, Mommy! Can we go now?"

Your child is not old enough to make decisions on her own, but some parents are too busy or lazy to parent their children and make those decisions for them. It is unbelievable, but some parents are afraid of upsetting their children and making them angry, so they give in, and their children will take advantage of that.

If your child whines and says, "Can we go now? Why not?" you should calmly say, "The answer is no. Not until I say it is time to go."

You do not have to explain why and you do not have to give a definite time for when you will be leaving. *Be Still & Be Quiet* Good Parenting 101 teaches that as the parent, you decide when you will leave.

If you start when your child is three or four, as they get older, you will get the response you want from them simply by the mere mention of the switch. Carrying a switch in your hand when out in public should be the only deterrent you need against disobedience and not listening to you as you take a walk in the neighborhood, to the park, to the drugstore, or to a friend's house.

Be Still & Be Quiet believes you will demonstrate your effectiveness at disciplining your child by her cooperation and helpful behavior, her relatedness to you, her willingness to listen to you, and her desire to please you and stay out of trouble.

Today's children, and some parents, are overwhelmed with modern day technology and information acceleration. You want to find out what your child is interested in and keep her busy. A child who is busy with positive activities is more likely to stay out of trouble as she reaches adolescence. You do not need to give your child too many choices at a young age. No toddler should decide whether to eat her vegetables, take medicine, or drink water instead of soda. What does a toddler know about health and dehydration?

Chapter 15

The Look and the Stance

Before your child enters pre-school or kindergarten, it is crucial for success that you have discouraged and intercepted behavior problems with good parenting and good discipline. If you, for whatever reason, have not disciplined your child at home, enforced being still and being quiet, or taught your child to follow directions, there are solutions by schools for the undisciplined child. One solution is that the school might need, for the safety of all present, i.e., the teacher, the child, other children, to have your child tested for ADD (Attention deficit disorder); or, ADHD (Attention deficit hyperactivity.) ADD is generally diagnosed for children who have short attention span and have a difficult time with concentration. ADHD has added hyperactivity or "bouncing off the wall" type behavior. Once tested by a professional, if diagnosed with one of these disorders, mental health counseling and possibly medication might be needed.

If you are a right thinking parent, you have taken the time at home to get past all the crying and screaming, the temper tantrums, and the meltdowns and done what is best for your child's well-being in preparation for his future. You know that by creating house rules and exercising consistent discipline, your child will be prepared for preschool and beyond. During his first five years, your child should have learned to recognize when you have reached the limits of your patience by a certain nonverbal communication called the look. *"The look"* means, "Not another word and you know what behavior I expect from you right now, not later."

Another corrective measure is going deep and adding bass to your voice. *Bass* in your authoritative voice means, "Do not test me. That is enough." It also means, "There is no argument that I want to hear."

Finally, there is *"the stance,"* which carries the same "Do not try my patience" message. The stance might be when you put your hand on your hip or cross your arms across your chest and glare at your child.

The look is the most powerful. Seeing the "I have reached my limit look" or "That's the last straw look," your son should adjust his behavior appropriately and obey directives willingly. When your child has learned to obey the rules at home, he will be on his best behavior at school and in public as well. He will have no desire to challenge your long distance authority. With no ongoing power struggles, life is a joy for all. This then is win-win behavior and a job well done. You now have become the good parent with the good child. A child who everyone is happy to see coming, talk with, and interact with.

A story regarding the look comes from the Father of a seven year old boy who was acting up at a campout and testing his Father's patience. The Father got out of his chair and assumed the stance position. He called his son, stared at him, and pointed his index finger to his forehead, an indication that his son needed to pay attention and think about his actions. As the son walked away from his Father to go play, he looked back and said in a clear and calm voice, "I know Dad, I know." The child acknowledged that his Father had his attention and that he would stop his annoying behavior. All at the campout who heard and saw this exchange was impressed.

If you have this behavior by your son, it is because you have worked on it at home. Therefore, you will get the same results in public. To summarize it all, with patience, corrections, and working with your child consistently at home, utilizing the look, the bass in your voice, and the stance, appropriate behavior should be expected in public just like it is expected at home.

Chapter 16

Parenting Wisely

Most parents in the United States of America and around the world are working hard every day and struggling to keep their children on track, on task, focused, productive, disciplined, and respectful. To the parents, the experts in child development have said that your children have "rights" and they are correct. Children do have rights. They have the right to be loved and nurtured. Children have the right to have their basic needs met. They have the right to be protected and live in and grow up in a safe home. Children have the right to be guided, taught and trained in teachable moments. Children have the right to expect parents to parent them so they do not have to parent themselves.

Parents have rights as well. They have the right to be listened to and respected at all times by their children. Parents have the right to have their house rules obeyed. Parents know that in their home no bedroom is "off limits" to them. They have the right to enter, look around and question undesirable items and clothes. Parents have the right to instruct and discipline their children. The parent rights come before their child's rights. Children whether three or eighteen are not your equal and should not be treated as if they are your equal.

Scenario #1

At a bus stop, you overhear a 12 year old telling his friend that his Mother had agreed for the two of them to get a good night's sleep after an argument and that they would discuss their problem with each other in the morning. Say what? You normally should make a decision about a problem with your child sooner rather than later. Otherwise, you are waiting on what? Sleep? Seriously?

If he and his Mother had argued, it must have been for a significant reason. Would she really have wanted to go to sleep if the argument was about stealing, vandalism, fighting, doing drugs, drinking alcohol, disrespecting a teacher or an elder?

Regarding everyday minor situations in the home. A Mother does not have to wait for her husband to come home to handle a troublesome situation. A Father should not have to wait for his wife to come home to deal with an infraction of the rules. If you need to calm down, put yourself in a time-out. To delay until morning or another time is to allow for manipulation by your child with a different and inconsistent outcome whereby in the end you usually do nothing.

Scenario #2

It seems that earlier that night, the Mother had gone to the son's friend's house to get her son, who had overstayed his request to visit. The Mother did not want to create a scene at the host's house, so she made a deal with her son in order to keep the peace and get the child in the car. The deal made was this, "Everything is forgiven. Let's just go home." Are you serious? Parents should never get into the habit of making deals with their child that entail looking the other way and disregarding negative or irresponsible behavior.

This is worth repeating. Do not make deals with your child regarding absurd behavior by ignoring or postponing consequences to some future time. Your child will hope that by postponing the discipline, you will get over being upset and drop the whole situation until the next time. Remember that all lack of action and follow-through suits your child just fine. But what has your child learned? He has learned how to manipulate you and not have to accept responsibility or suffer consequences for his mannish behavior. Who is the boss of whom?

If you ask little of your child, you will receive little from him, especially when he is older. This means you will get little respect, little consideration, little empathy, and little help from your child when you are older.

When giving directives or making requests of your child, be specific. Do not generalize what you are telling your child to do. Follow-up by checking to make sure that what you instructed or asked him to do has been done. If this sounds like policing your child in the home, so be it. Obedience is the key to thoughtfulness, cooperation, and love. With your son's compliance, you are instilling in him a solid foundation for character building and moral ethics.

To pretend you didn't notice your child did not do as directed is to harm your relationship in so many unseen ways. Disobedience starts with forgetfulness, excuses, neglect, and a lack of cooperation. It progresses to opposition, defiance, and outright resentment. When you tell your child to do something, it needs to be done without complaining, arguing, debating, and delaying; or else, there are consequences.

This is not asking too much of your child. Again, if you ask little of your child, then little will be given to you later on. He will never volunteer to help you do the smallest task. Therefore, ask your son to bring you a glass of water on a regular basis, then it becomes no big deal. The same applies to having your child give you a kiss or a hug. It is normalized as what we do every day, not just on birthdays or holidays.

If you parent in a lackadaisical fashion, it is guaranteed that your child will do little that you ask. Children 12 or older will challenge you the very next morning by asking, "Why are you bringing up last night's argument or incident?" Or they might look at you and innocently ask, "Why do you keep talking about old stuff?" By doing nothing after you give your child a directive, this is the beginning of a losing battle for the parent who allows this to occur.

If your child is going through a difficult time at home, with his peers, or at school, you might need to take a day off from work to spend time with him. It will be beneficial for both of you because it will show him that you are paying attention to his difficulties and support him. So take a step back from your daily routine and contemplate what your child's problem might be and discuss it with him. It will be time well spent together. You will communicate with each other, reconnect, and build mutual trust as you attempt to help solve the problem or difficulty.

Chapter 17

Ask Amy

Have you ever wondered, who makes a good parent? "Ask Amy" newspaper column addressed that question as it concerned a teenage daughter who was acting out. Amy scolded a "Furious Mom" who had burned her daughter's "trashy fashion magazines." The Mother had lost it and had burned the magazines due to the daughter's disobedience at home and at school regarding the magazines. She received phone calls from the school that the magazines were being confiscated routinely because the teen was reading them in class instead of paying attention to the teacher. The Mother was also reacting to her teen calling the teacher a "bitch."

Prior to burning the magazines, the Mother warned her daughter that her actions were forcing her to react. She did this when she told her daughter, "Something is going to happen to your magazines that you won't like."

In the advice column, Amy advised the Mother to show positive, pro-social behavior even when a child is acting out. Say what? Amy suggested that the Mother talk to her daughter to find out what she liked about the magazines. Did she like the clothes? Did she like the magazines' racy content? Did she like the way the models looked or posed? Did she admire the confidence the models seemed to have?

Amy further suggested a meeting with the teacher to discuss her daughter's challenges and disrespectful behavior. The Mother was told to ask for the teacher's recommendation.

Be Still & Be Quiet would like you to ponder this! Why is this the teacher's problem? Why does the teachers have to come up with a recommendation? The teacher should not have to solve a problem this child created.

Teachers have to be in control of their classroom. Parents have to be in control of and teach their children appropriate behavior. Calling the teacher a "bitch" is not appropriate. It is the parents' job to keep their children in line through home training and discipline.

Because the child defied and disrespected the teacher, the challenge for the parent was to hold her daughter accountable for negative and unacceptable behavior. Since the child created the problem, she should be encouraged to come up with a solution. Most teens are capable of coming up with a satisfactory solution given the opportunity. To expect less of her is equivalent to her Mother saying her daughter was incapable of problem solving.

Let us say the Mother has a calm discussion with her daughter as "Ask Amy" suggested, no yelling and no drama. The parent could attempt to find out why the child did what she did. A calm discussion should result in the daughter realizing that she owed the teacher an apology because she had challenged and cursed her.

Once this parent has gotten her child to apologize for calling the teacher a "bitch," she will have to address the problem of her daughter not paying attention in class with a relevant consequence. A parent should not give up on her child, but she should not give in to her foolishness either.

Obviously, the child cannot continue to read trashy magazines in the classroom or anywhere else. In a nurturing manner, this Mother could look at magazine options for her young lady. There are fashion, modeling, and glamour magazines. The Mother could allow for one or two subscriptions to more appropriate magazines such as *Essence*, *Cosmopolitan*, or *O, the Oprah* magazine.

Chapter 18

Concerned Parent vs. Spy

What does it mean to be a concerned parent vs spy? Does it mean that the parent is not allowed in her teenager's bedroom because it is off limits? This goes back to individuality and personhood. Should your child have a lock on her door that prevents you from having access so that you can observe what she has in her room due to some notion of privacy? Until and unless your daughter is paying rent, no room in your house should be off limits to you. No computer is off limits, nor should your child shut it down as you come into a room. If a bedroom door is locked and that is not your wish, take the door off its hinges. This, as a solution, should not be necessary in a calm, trusting, and loving household.

Here is an example of what you might say to your daughter on the subject of you looking in and possibly searching her room with or without her being present. "It is my duty as a caring parent to know what's going on in our home. I am checking drawers, looking under the bed, and any place in your room that I want to check. I am checking for anything that should not be there, drugs, alcohol, gang paraphernalia, or weapons."

If she asks, "Why?" your answer is, "Because I am the parent and I am building our home on a solid foundation. This is what God wants in order for Him to protect our happy home. Furthermore, as your parent, I refuse to allow you to disrespect me by telling me what I should be doing, talking back to me, not listening to me, and mumbling about a directive I give you. I will not tolerate your mouth being poked out, rolling your eyes in defiance, hateful stares, or hurtful words said to me such as, 'I hate you' or any other form of ungodly behavior. In this house, we will have obedience, order, thoughtfulness, listening and showing respect. We will live in a Godly manner because where confusion is, God is not."

Teach your Child Internet Safety

Your challenge as a parent will be to monitor your child's online activities. There is clear danger on the internet, so monitoring it is essential. To keep your child safe, you need to be informed. This is not being overprotective.

A couple of ways to get involved with your child's internet use is to work on a strong password together and develop an identifier for proof of the user's identity. What is your child's user name? You are a concerned parent who needs to know.

If your child is computer savvy and on the internet, ask for her help in setting up your own Facebook (messenger), Twitter, Instagram, or YouTube account. That way, you can test how computer literate your child has become. When the opportunity presents itself, take a

Facebook training workshop or read the book *Facebook for Dummies*. Sometimes, a library or job coalition agency will offer social media workshops for free.

From time to time, discuss Facebook and other social media where applicable with your child. You can also send an occasional link to a funny YouTube video to your daughter. This will help you to bond with her and remind her that you are active and alert as to what goes on online.

As a concerned parent, educate your child regarding physical bullying as well as "cyberbullying" others. *Cyberbullying* means "Using computers or other electronic devices to disrespect and make hurtful comments about another, to lie to others in an attempt to destroy someone's reputation, and/or to intimidate and threaten others."

Parents can research for tips and information on cyber-safety programs. A good website to visit is cybersafesoft.com. Cyber-safety programs use encryption software designed to keep your child safe while on the internet. Do supervise your child's computer usage. Your own knowledge and awareness is the key to keeping your child safe.

Educate your child against "sexting" anyone at any time. *Sexting* involves, "Sending nude or semi-nude pictures of yourself on social media." The dangers of sexting are many including the possibility of victimization because a child could easily be blackmailed to do things she does not want to do. She could also receive bullying messages. There is also the embarrassment in the future, as an adult, of having used bad judgment or engaged in questionable or despicable behavior when younger. Sexting can present issues with college acceptance, employment, and future relationships.

Smartphones, tablets, and other electronic devices are another concern for parents. *Be Still & Be Quiet* suggests that you be proactive and vigilant. A five or eight year old does not need a Smartphone, iPhone, iPad, et cetera.

Trending in some communities is a movement to encourage parents to hold off on giving their children smartphones until the eighth grade. Their pledge is "Wait Until 8th" grade. The idea behind it is that smartphones and tablets are distracting, dangerous, and detrimental to young children's health. The aim is to have several families from a classroom sign a pledge for strength in numbers, as well as decreased pressure, and as a push back to any negativity regarding the "Wait Until 8th for internet access. Why wait? I'm glad you asked! Smartphones contribute towards poor academics and poor sleep patterns. Children will sometimes get up in the middle of the night, unbeknownst to their parent and play games or watch YouTube until 1:00 or 2:00 am, especially on the weekend.

It has been reported on TV that the country of France is banning Smartphones from their elementary schools. These trends are food for thought, no doubt!

Children are often spending anywhere between three to six hours daily in front of a screen. This means spending three hours plus in isolation, snapchatting, instagramming, and watching YouTube.

Why are children becoming addicted to their devices? It's being called, a fear of missing out (FOMO). This fear is causing genuine concerns regarding addictions. In the future, think detox centers for "techno junkies."

Regarding future health concerns, imagine eight year olds, or younger children, holding their heads down for up to three hours a day looking at their cellphone or a tablet placed on a desk or resting on her lap. There is a new name for what medical condition their neck may develop in the future. It is called, "Tech Neck." This is new stuff. There is much to be researched and understood regarding this new medical dilemma. What can you do right now for your adolescent? First, monitor and allow your child a limited amount of time on electronics. Too much of anything is always harmful. Second, teach her the importance of holding her Smartphone, iPhone iPad, and Tablet at eye level, each and every time when using these devices.

As a ninth grader and the older child in the home, Felipe has access to the family's Smartphone while his six year old brother does not. Felipe has been instructed and has learned to always remove all cellphones from the table at dinner time.

Be Still & Be Quiet recommends that one of your house rules should be at a designated time your oldest child, which in this case is Felipe, should also put away the Smartphones and Tablets in preparation for bedtime.

As a proactive parent, encourage your children during the day to turn off the electronics and instead interact with nature by going outside, creating a food or flower garden, watering the grass, raking the leaves, taking a walk with friends, playing soccer or some other sport.

Families can plan day trips to the closest National State Park to enjoy the magic of nature. Nature is learning where our water and food comes from. A blue mountain is not really blue. As you get up close and personal, that same mountain is now brown. If you can't go outdoors, you have indoor fun with board games; such as, chess, dominoes, puzzles, and card games to play with.

On the subject of the Smartphone, there are apps that allow parents to control when their children can and cannot use their smartphones. Additionally, parents can learn what apps are available to their children. Again, a parent's job is to be proactive which means setting limits and boundaries ahead of time.

Chapter 19

Permissiveness

Permissiveness or spoiling your child results in great spiritual, physical, and emotional harm to him. Such damage could result in your son never recovering from a feeling of entitlement for the rest of his life. Permissiveness corrupts the soul by the individual becoming narcissistic, selfish, self-centered, and having a self-absorbed nature, not to mention a lack of empathy, sympathy, and Godly beliefs.

Permissiveness can spoil your child physically if it means he can eat whenever and whatever he want. Obesity could lead to childhood diabetes. Permissiveness can cause emotional immaturity and creates an attitude of dependence. A child of permissive parents can easily become a poor team player with poor social and people skills. This could lead to the bullying of others.

Crying to get your way starts in the toddler years and spills over into the preschool and kindergarten years. As your child grows, such crybaby behavior becomes frustrating to all care givers of the child. When your child goes to visit relatives his screaming and crying when he cannot get what he wants, will cause all present to wish him gone. Permissiveness amounts to poor parenting no matter how it is justified, rationalized, or minimized.

A "Hands-off" parenting style is the same as permissiveness. A "Hands-off" style might be a Mother who is uninvolved and who sets no boundaries for her child. This is a child with few limitations on behavior at home and who will go out into the world ill prepared with his permissive attitude. Starting with elementary school, permissiveness rears its ugly head as entitled, rude, disrespectful, boasting and arrogant.

And this is just the beginning. As the years pass, a child's lack of socialization skills and the ability to talk fairly to people can cause the child to not listen to adults in authority, and not follow societal rules. Overindulging and spoiling your child is the slow kiss of death to your relationship with him. More often than not, he will parent the parent by dictating what he wants and how quickly he wants it. If the parent now wants to refuse to comply with his demands, the line is drawn in the sand, and the war between the parent and the child begins.

Again, if permissiveness is your parenting style and you continue in this vein until your child is an adolescent, do not be surprise if his behavior at home and school has gotten worse. Are you surprised? You should not be, because permissiveness promotes negative behavior. In the old days, folks used to say, "The handwriting was on the wall!"

What will happen if your adolescent child is never given instructions to pick up after himself? What if he has never been taught to ask for things politely, rather than in a demanding manner? What if this same child was never required to be obedient and respectful and say, "Please" and "thank you"? What if he walks around all day with an "I don't care" attitude?

Suppose your son was never taught to show appreciation for gifts received? How about never showing compassion for people; nor, animals suffering or dying. What we are talking about is that you, the parent, will receive failing grades for not teaching family values, respect for self and others, and compassion for those less fortunate. Permissive parenting produces children with poor people skills and an unacceptable, aggressive, and even violent nature.

More and more these days, children and young adults are easily angered, stressed, disconnected, spiteful, revengeful, and depressed. They call their peers nasty names and frequently get into arguments and fights. Children often talk back to aunts and uncles and walk away even when their parent is talking to them. They curse and argue with their teachers, principal, and even the police.

Children are in trouble today because they follow unruly peers, drink alcohol, smoke, eat or drink editable marijuana, take drugs, jump into gangs, wear gang attire or sagging pants, do drive-by shootings, and do not follow rules. They are frequently suspended or expelled from school. Children are often mean spirited. Additionally, children have too much time on their hands which gets them into trouble with the law which often leads to detainment at juvenile hall, or, at 18 or older, in jail.

This same child is said to have autonomy, independence, personhood, and a lack of inhibition. The fact is that often, no one wants to deal with such a child not even if he is yours. People would rather see him walking away from them; rather than, see him coming towards them.

The truth be told, what Mother, Father, family member, friend, or teacher would be surprised by the bad behavior of a child who has been given too many choices, too many privileges, and too much stuff from age two to the present? This is a child who has been given the power of parenting himself while his parents sat back and watched this train wreck happen.

Children who are the "shot callers" and who parent themselves for an extended period of time, will in all likelihood become frustrated, have anger issues, and maybe even depression, because that should not be their job. Children want more than anything for parents to parent them. It is likely that their future wife or husband may have hell to pay in their marriage due to isolation, a lack of nurturing, hugs and kisses referred to by mental health counselors as "abandonment issues." A husband diagnosed with a narcissistic personality disorder shows contempt and a total disregard for the feelings of his wife and others.

In another worst-case scenario, you suspect your teenager is sexually active and having unprotected sex and has possibly contracted a sexually transmitted disease (STD). You have your fingers crossed that he doesn't get the girl pregnant. At some point, you do have to talk to your son about abstaining from sex or at the very least using protection. Hopefully, he will be mature enough to listen to your concerns during this very serious conversation.

You should discuss with your son your hopes and dreams for him. You could offer rewards and incentives that have worked in the past to curb his behavior. Some public schools offer sex education and that will reinforce what you have already educated him on and cautioned him about.

Is your child running away from home the biggest problem in your household? Running away could be due to peer pressure. You should definitely know who your child's friends are and where they live. Introduce yourself to each of your son's friends and meet their parents as soon as possible.

Let us return to the topic of marijuana, there is some question about whether daily smoking marijuana is a harmful drug. Studies suggest that adolescents' and teenagers' developing brains are more susceptible to harm from smoking marijuana than are adults' brains. It is a fact that the human brain is not fully developed until the midtwenties. Studies suggest that regular use of this drug in youth leads to a permanent decrease in IQ. Research has indicated that daily users of marijuana can have a greater risk of developing psychosis.

Daily use of marijuana is harmful to the health and well-being of adolescents, teenagers, and young adults. Should your child get arrested for drug possession that will be a sad sight to see, you and other Mothers hugging their sons in juvenile hall or jail. Throughout this parental guideline, do your own investigation to confirm what is being said or suggested regarding marijuana use and abuse.

Again, does your child know your expectations of him? Have you ever sat down calmly at the kitchen table and reviewed with your child what you expect? Appropriate parenting includes teaching children your expectations for them at home, school, and elsewhere.

Not that long ago families, extended families, and neighbors were connected physically, spiritually, and emotionally. The mantra, "It takes a village to raise a child" was the belief of the day.

Some parents need to be less permissive and more diligent in their no-nonsense teachings, training, protecting, and nurturing of their children to maximize their healthy development. Is this you?

Chapter 20

A Good Parent

What then is the definition of a good parent? A good parent takes her young child by the hand when out and about which gives the child a feeling of security. A sight to see is a 10 year old daughter holding her Mother's hand as they walk across the street. A good parent will guide, instruct, protect, and teach her child in the way she should go in life. A healthy household functions with daily prayer to God and displays of love and affection. This is a home that instills hope, validates efforts, and gives lots of praise and encouragement to the children living there.

Single Mothers or Fathers will have to wear both hats and perform both roles. This is very hard, but it can be made easier with the help of your extended family, which would be your brother, sister, grandparents, uncle, aunt, cousin, or best friend.

In your two parent household consisting of a Father and Mother, they should operate as a team. Your child should not be able to go from one parent to the other to get what she wants through manipulation. Also, all parents should know that they do not have to explain or justify a directive given to their child.

Good parents help their daughter with learning age appropriate behavior before she even goes to preschool or Head Start. Good parents are not willing to let their children challenge or ignore their decisions. Good parents are firm but fair. Good parents are a little obsessive-compulsive when it comes to being obeyed by their children. Each child is different. What works for one child might not work for another child. In any case, parents need to be fair, firm, and flexible, have understanding and patience.

Be Still & Be Quiet suggest that as the parent, you should know if your child is courteous, thoughtful, of high morals, and of noble virtue. Your daughter needs good people skills. This means knowing how to talk respectfully to all adults especially females, who are disrespected more often than males. Your child should exhibit a friendly personality. She should never demean or call her classmates names, no bullying and no fighting.

Engage your daughter in daily conversations about school. Involve her in whatever is going on in the home and with the family. She should know your expectations. You should have open, honest, relaxed, and respectful communication with each other.

Once your child is in school, attend parent/teacher conferences and open houses. Make sure all electronic devices are turned off when your child is doing homework unless a computer or particular device is needed to complete the homework. If you eliminate distractions, your child will develop good study habits early on. With a consistent study time, study environment, and with your help when needed, your child should not fall behind in her studies. Bad study habits could lead to low self-esteem and academic failure.

Your child needs eight to ten hours of sleep each night. A TV left on in the bedroom at bedtime is not conducive to a good night's sleep. A night-light should be sufficient for any fear of the dark. Remember, house rules and practices are not up for debate or argument.

From preschool to high school, with your discipline and guidance, your child will not have an "I don't care" attitude about her education and the school she attends. She will have school pride. Although it is not mandated by the school district, *Be Still & Be Quiet* suggests that all parents meet with their child's teachers in all grades to assist in parent and teachers' expectations. Teachers report often feeling disconnected and feeling a sense of disengagement between them and parents. It is not uncommon for a teacher to feel isolated and operating in a vacuum with them fighting their school district's administration for the sake of the children. If necessary, parents should joint venture with teachers to put on workshops that address issues and concerns involving the school and its policies.

The 15 NO's

This is how an entire generation of youngsters will manage to be courteous and respectful when given the right guidance; and, when it comes to obeying God, parents, teachers, authority, adults, the elderly, the environment, and society.

- No sagging pants, use a belt, and wear pants that fit
- No baggy pants two sizes too big
- No talking back, smacking lips, rolling eyes, glaring, or staring
- No walking away when an adult is talking to you
- No cursing, pushing, or hitting an adult or elder **ever**
- No blasting loud music in your car that will make you deaf one day
- No shoes thrown across an overhead wire to identify a drug neighborhood
- No vandalism, graffiti or defacing public statures or buildings
- No calling a female (who is someone's Mother, daughter, sister, niece) a bitch or a whore
- No disrespect for or destroying others' property
- No running away from home
- No vaping, flavored e-cigarettes with kiddy names, alcohol, and drug use
- No bullying others
- No joining a gang
- No refusal to bathe/shower because cleanliness is next to godliness

Be Still & Be Quiet is not suggesting you deny Katrina's creativity or identity, which is tied to her self-esteem. Sagging and oversized baggy pants are not a sign of individuality but rather a sign of rebellion and disregard for what others think. Your teenager should not get a tattoo without your permission. Katrina should not be allowed to dress in ways that do not reflect your family values; no outrageous heavy makeup, no gang clothes, red or blue bandannas, or anything negative that signals a gang lifestyle.

Continue to mold your child to grow in confidence, creativity, and cooperation. Nothing feels better to your daughter than to be at the right place and doing the right thing at the right time, and in harmony with her surroundings at home or in public. Children get that early on if they are taught to recognize fair and reasonable self-expression, self-awareness, and self-control, the three selves.

Chapter 21

Promote Independence

Parents will decide for their household at what age of maturity to begin encouraging their child's freedom of expression and opinion.

In your effort to promote independence, you ask, "When should my child have a voice as well as choices and opinions?" *Be Still & Be Quiet* suggests that you give your child some autonomy at about nine years old. This is when you can begin asking your child for his input into what he wants to wear to school; what food he would prefer to eat; and, what rewards he would like to have after he has completed his chores. Around eight or nine year old, you can motivate and help your child with thinking about and writing down obtainable, age appropriate goals. You will be able to discuss his fears, hopes, and dreams.

Be Still & Be Quiet wishes to encourage you to teach your child through role playing and modeling the behavior you desire in your son. Role playing is to discuss, let us say, your son's fear of embarrassing himself perhaps by spilling milk all over his pants in the cafeteria. He could practice using humor and make jokes about his predicament. Another example might be that he did not make it to the restroom in time and peed on himself. Help your son to see his self as okay. Roleplay his actions after his accident. Also, what will he do to prevent this situation from occurring again? He might need to get the teacher's attention sooner in order to ask for permission to leave the classroom. He might need to leave sooner and not wait an extra 10 minutes debating with himself when to ask for permission to leave.

When you are giving directives to your child, keep it simple and be specific. Your child will need to pay attention to develop good listening skills and learn through acting out skits.

If you have the desire and the time to instruct and teach good listening skills, try the infamous, "Peter Piper picked a peck of pickled peppers. A peck of pickled peppers Peter Piper picked. If Peter Piper picked a peck of pickled peppers, where is the peck of pickled peppers Peter Piper picked?" Make the training and the learning fun because the two of you will benefit by making this love connection on the road to independence and self-determination.

Here is something for parents to think about.

"Attitudes"

The longer I live, the more I realize the importance
of choosing the right attitude in life.
Attitude is more important than facts.
It is more important than your past;
more important than your education or financial situation;
more important than your circumstances, your successes, or your failures;
more important than what other people think, say or do.
It is more important than appearance, your giftedness, or your skills.
It will make or break a company. It will cause a church to soar or sink.
It will make the difference between a happy home or a miserable home.
You have a choice each day regarding the attitude you will embrace.
Life is like a violin.
You can focus on the broken strings that dangle,
or you can play your life's melody on the one that remains.
You cannot change the years that have passed,

nor can you change the daily tick of the clock.

You cannot change the pace of your march toward your death.

You cannot change the decisions or reactions of other people.

And you certainly cannot change the inevitable.

Those are strings that dangle!

What you can do is play on the one string that remains—your attitude.

I am convinced that life is 10 percent what happens to me

and 90 percent how I react to it.

The same is true for you.

— Chuck Swindoll1

If you have a good attitude, most likely, your child will have a good attitude because young children are sponges. They imitate their parents' reactions and coping skills regarding the good and the bad things that happen at home. We all know that bad things happen to good people. How parents react to situations and especially tragic ones demonstrates the glue that strengthens the families' in coming together.

Children tend to behave and talk like their parents. Your child will be an imitation of you. If you are too busy to be helpful, too busy to listen, and too busy to engage in family fun activities with your child, he will grow up to be too busy for you with his own children. You are the blueprint for your family's beliefs. Do work with your child in drafting a plan for implementing hopes, goals, and dreams. Encourage your son to sign up for summer leadership programs in his pursuit for independence training.

Be a role model for the person you want your child to be. You must be a living day-to-day example of your values, attitude, integrity, gratefulness, compassion, honesty, generosity, and willingness to help others who are less fortunate.

Chapter 22

Less Clutter Equals Less Stress

Be Still & Be Quiet recommends that instead of a TV, PlayStation, or computer in your child's bedroom, all three belong in an all-purpose room or den.

TVs, computers, and electronic gadgetries have become today's babysitter. A typical home will turn on the TV early in the morning whether or not anyone is watching it. If no one is watching the TV, it becomes background noise. The TV is then left on until the last member of the house goes to bed. The next day it starts all over again.

Children, especially those from three to eleven, need peaceful and quiet homes. A child with too many distractions will learn inattentiveness due to a stressful home environments. Too much noise, arguments, and clutter will cause your child to become unfocused, easily distracted, unruly, agitated, and uncooperative.

Children are also stressed out with too many choices, too many toys, to many electronics, too many after school activities and practices, too many rehearsals, and just too many things.

When you buy multiple pairs of expensive Lebrons or Air Yeezy sneakers, they lose their value in his eyes. If you buy Microsoft's Xbox Game Passes for his PlayStation, he will start feeling entitled to them and they will also lose their value for him.

Be Still & Be Quiet recommends you purchase only what you have money for. If you cannot afford an expensive name brand outfit or designer shoes, do not buy them. Do not ruin your budget or cause yourself stress by spending money you do not have.

A lot of choices means power. Children are given power while demanding more things. Things in the future might replace people and meaningful personal relationships. An accumulation of things can be emotionally draining. According to authors, Jeffrey Froh and Giacomo Bono, "Less is more." Today's parents would do well to develop this concept.

When homework is worked on, turn off the TV, CD player, phone, and the radio. Children benefit from the removal of unnecessary noise and overwhelming clutter of their minds, emotions, and physical well-being.

Today's accelerated pace of life and overstimulation especially due to technology appears to be the new "rite of passage." It dictates more techno toys at a younger and younger age. This means there are fewer and fewer traditional age-appropriate toys. Technology for young children is a powerful distraction when it comes to learning good socialization and age-appropriate communication skills. Young people whose minds and emotions are overstimulated suffer from confused thinking, information overload, anxiety, and fatigue.

Children as young as five are receiving cellphones and tablets. Thus begins the clutter of the mind, of the emotions, and of the ability to talk with confidence, not shy, and not with delayed speech. Children will sit with heads down looking at their devices. They mumble when they talk and exhibit delayed speech. Sensory stimulation overload has symptoms of irritability, refusal to participate in activities and/or interact with others. Additional, symptoms of disconnect from people are poor eye contact, avoidance of touching and being touched.

Watching any kind of screen for a long time, which could be up to 3 hours and more, teaches your child to be passive, isolated, distracted, and detached. Additionally, one or both parents need to monitor how much time is spent watching TV and playing computer games, especially due the violent nature of some TV shows and video games.

The American Academy of Pediatrics has sounded the alarm that young children are especially vulnerable to physical damage from cellphone radiation and should not use cellphones at all, or for limited amounts of time. Radiation standards in cellphones and other wireless devices have been proposed to the Federal Communications Commission (FCC) for reassessment.

Additionally, the American Academy of Pediatrics suggested that other than the occasional cartoon, children younger than 18 months should be completely unplugged. Teachers are seeing children entering preschool, kindergarten, and first grade unable to clearly communicate for their age level. They are instead, mumbling, with heads down, shy, confused, withdrawn, fearful, and introverted.

Parents should limit their children's choices and prevent their being overstimulated to protect them while they are developing. This can mean keeping your child from seeing commercials that businesses aim directly at him and are meant to appeal to his wishes and desires. Parents should say no to commercials that glamorize products because happiness does not come from a vast amount of toys, large screen games, and other commercial technology.

Happiness comes primarily from human relationships, relationships with animals, and a one-on-one connection with nature; hikes in the wood, climbing hills and mountains, fishing in streams and lakes, and boating while wearing lifejackets.

And now parents have a new concern regarding mental health. Intense video game players can become addicted after hours and hours of playing on a daily basis. Future diagnosis might be called, "gaming disorder." This is new and disturbing for our current and future generation of young people. It is real and it is serious. Point to remember, too much of anything is not good for you.

Parents, teachers, and counselors might initially see ADD or ADHD when in fact your child is simply stressed by clutter. When stressed, your child might display inattentive, disorganized, unruly, antsy, hyperactive, uncooperative, argumentative, disobedient, oppositional, or aggressive. Please consult your child's pediatrician for an accurate diagnosis should you have concerns regarding your child's behavior. The earlier the diagnosis the better.

Children need playtime, outdoor time, and quiet time to think. Relationships need to be worked on during quiet time because connectedness with your child can sometimes falter. Connecting with each other needs to be prioritized and the rebuilding of a child's spirit worked on. In a few words, "Slow down because speed kills". Children become anxious when you hurry them. Children become stressed when they feel overloaded with choices, places to go, and things to accomplish. A child could act out with violence if the stress becomes too great. Less clutter equals less stress.

Children are living, breathing, wonderful human beings that we need to take notice of. One way is to engage your child by asking him open-ended questions about his day that require more than a yes or no answer. This means less time with techno gadgetry and more time with family and friends. In that same vein, playfulness, spontaneous and creative play will cause your child to use his imagination in make believe games with you, his sibling, or playmate.

Parents, teach your child what is important in life such as family and real friends. Children between five and ten years old do not need the latest "must have" toys or games to be "one up" on the neighbor's kid. Technology can sometimes rob a young child of their innocence. Seriously! Does a seven year old really need the use of his personal cellphone to be the highlight of his day?

Do the work. Work on having a calm home. A home is calm if it is absent of constant stimulation, loud noise, or constant background noise, and clutter. Your child will respond to a calm environment in a positive way with less volatility and negativity. With a calm and quiet home, all inappropriate behavior should be reduced to allow for teachable moments. There should be fewer arguments and aggressive behavior, which is then replaced with improved coping skills, willing to try, and improved attitude in this relaxed atmosphere.

Your son will demonstrate more awareness of people in and outside the home. This is a good time to work on family values, praying together, helping around the home, assisting the elderly, working on individual projects, or taking care of the pet. Ideally, some or all of this is doable.

Consideration should be given to your child to allow for alone time in their room, elsewhere in the home, or the backyard. Cooler than that! How about unstructured and unscheduled time? Sometimes the best time is having nothing to do time. Allow your child to be bored, he will figure out something to do to entertain himself.

Facebook (messenger), Snapchat, Twitter, and Instagram are designed to steal your child's childhood. How? I am glad you asked! This technology is programmed to become all day entertainment in an electrical, non-human relationship. If left unsupervised, your child will be consumed by these internet devices. He will be left with an attention span of next to none. Curiosity for people and adventure in the outside world will be of little importance. Feelings for the human touch, verbal communication and memorable experiences of little value.

Technology for your little one too soon can be devilish. A parent has the responsibility to rebuke the devil and his goods in the name of the Lord. We all need intimacy, friendship, and trust of others. That comes through honest communication and feeling others happiness and pain. The cellphone or tablet a parent gives a small child will encourage that child to stop working on his verbal and interpersonal skills, as well as imagination.

Be Still & Be Quiet recommends that you say to no one in particular, "The devil is a liar." Then get busy and unplug your youngster from social media. When you can do so in good conscience, give age-appropriate electronics to your child. Make sure he is mature enough and the purpose is there, to use the technology responsibly. As the parent, you make the final decisions for your family.

Chapter 23

No-Kids Zone

The latest trend in some dining restaurants is to have a "No Kids Zone" that excludes anyone six years old or younger. In such restaurants, they have a policy, "We reserve the right to refuse service to anyone, including children." Some parents like this idea while others do not.

This trend does not include family restaurants. McDonald's, Burger King, Popeye's, and other well-known establishments will always be, welcoming, family friendly, and fun for children.

Chris Shake, owner of Old Fisherman's Grotto, a popular tourist eatery on Fisherman's Wharf in Monterey, California, has had for years a no-noisy children policy. A sign reads, "No Strollers, No High Chairs, and No Booster Chairs. Children crying or making loud noises are a distraction to other diners and as such are not allowed in the dining room."

Shake stated, "At Old Fisherman's Grotto, we strive to give all of our guests the best dining experience possible. The policy relating to children was put in place to enhance the experience of all our diners with and without children."

Be Still & Be Quiet agrees with this trend and wants all parents to know that the same idea holds true for airplane flights. Do have something for your child to play with during the flight so he does not disturb others. It goes back again to teaching children at a very young age to be respectful and have compassion for each other's needs. Because we really are our "brother's keeper." Too much individuality, isolation, disconnectedness, and disengagement is having a negative effect on everyone's quality of life, which used to be filled with consideration, being protective, kindness, and thoughtfulness for others.

Chapter 24

Education, Education, Education

Head Start is one option available to families whose income is primarily from agricultural work. A federal preschool program designed to help your three to five year old and get him ready for kindergarten. Head Start is a comprehensive child and family development program that offers education, health, nutrition, family support, transportation assistance, and disability services.

Head Start could begin with an instructor making weekly visits to your home with an early education program or your child could attend a local center. The home educator would help the parent who is the primary educator. The parent would learn how to teach Shawn age-appropriate basics of education while developing a sustainable and positive relationship with learning. Home based instruction for 60 to 90 minute per week is a precursor to Head Start, which targets three to five year olds in preparation for kindergarten. Proof of age with a birth certificate, income verification, and immunization records are a must. If you child has special needs, there may not be an income requirement.

Essentially, preschool and pre-K are the same. Both are introductions to making the transition to kindergarten. Your child must be ready for kindergarten. It is very important that Shawn has structure, discipline, and can Be Still & Be Quiet in order to hear the teacher teach. This entails good listening skills. There is also the skill of cooperation and following instruction.

Strive to get your child prepared for kindergarten before the first day of school. Take advantage of your school district's early education programs. Great futures for all children start in kindergarten.

An example of future educational services might be an observation booth at the back of the classroom that would allow a parent to step into the class unseen. The booth would have a one-way glass window where a Mom or Dad could observe their child's learning abilities and behavior without disrupting the class. The parent could pop in and out daily or as needed. Parents would also be encouraged to consider volunteering to be a room Mom or Dad.

Since the funding crisis years of the recession have ended, replaced by new, local Control Funding Formula laws, many school districts are reducing class sizes. Programs are coming back better than before including arts, music, drama, and dance, along with vigorous science and math programs.

Another possible example of future change might be designated schools allowing 30 additional compensated minutes of instructional time with students every day. This is the equivalent of 18 additional days a year in instructional hours to help children learn and excel.

A first grade teacher cannot teach a class with an out-of-control child. Perhaps it is your child who is unstructured, disobedient, rude, disrespectful, loud, and disruptive. This child is on a collision course with society and the rules of the land. To have no social skills or poor social skills is to miscue or make errors in judgment outside of normal and acceptable behavior. To miscue on what is appropriate and fair will keep a child on the outside looking in at others; and, on the road to becoming a misfit.

A good education with an early foundation in reading will allow your child to eventually go anywhere in the country or even the world that he wants to go to in life. A pivotal milestone is that by third grade, your child needs to be a third grade reader to accomplish success. With your help and the school providing the tools necessary, your son will benefit academically, socially, and emotionally. This nurturing can be compared to the nurturing you give to a plant or a puppy. Children also thrive and achieve when given parental love, hugs and kisses, guidance, and protection.

In high school and college, you want your child to be ready when opportunities become available. A good education is priceless.

Let us examine paying your child for good grades because some parents believe children should receive pay for that.

The pros might be as follows:

- It could stop kids from dropping out of school.
- It could be a hook to keep adolescents involved in school.
- It might help them not consider school boring and classroom work a waste of time.

The cons might be as follows:

- Children are taught to be money motivated instead of learning for its own reward.
- The perception might be that low-income students and students of color need extra incentives to do what is expected of them.
- Continual education pertains to school but also lifetime experience that go beyond the school.

Be Still & Be Quiet believes that through good parenting skills acquired over the years, parents will keep their children grounded and engaged in school. It is not the teachers' job. It is the parents' job. Therefore, you must decide between the pros and cons of paying your child to cooperate with you and complete chores as directed.

Do not allow your child to be tardy to preschool. He might start thinking that being tardy is no big deal and think that way all the way through high school. The long term harmful impact of your child missing school is real. The more times your child misses school unnecessarily, the more likely he will develop poor study habits and perform below grade level.

Tardy and unexcused absences create a snowball effect that will cause your child to struggle academically. If your son has holes in his academic education, it will affect his intellectual ability, self-esteem, attitude, cooperation, respect, and behavior. But tardiness of course does not include medical appointments, band dates, court hearings, and home emergencies.

During the school year, Quan, your seventh grader, will get up quickly each morning, shower, get dressed, and take completed homework for that day's school assignment. This means, not only completing homework but actually handing it in for a grade. Quan will walk with friends to school; or, you will drive him to school on time. Think about this, "to be on time is to be late" as in 10 seconds, 20 second, 30 seconds, one minute late, and so forth. So, in actuality, you want to be early rather than "on time." Get it! Got it! Good! Ha, ha!

Once he arrives at school, Quan will behave courteously and perform well in class. It is a parent's job to make sure that this is happening daily. Pop up at your son's school every now and then is a great idea.

All children need to read, read, and read some more. Reading, writing sentences, and paragraphs without help is the key to success by the third grade. Parents need to be vigilant about where their fifth and sixth graders and older children get their information for local and worldly news so they are not manipulated by unreliable, "fake" news.

If Quan has difficulties with reading and homework, you might find tutorial help at your child's school, libraries, or community centers. *Be Still & Be Quiet* promotes the belief that "anywhere you want to go in world, a good education and a good attitude will take you there."

Parents should expect their seventh and eighth graders to come home with A's and B's unless he has a medical or learning disability. Strict parents believe that academic pressure is good. Without pressure and high expectations, there will be no mastery of education and therefore no gifted child.

For some parents, it means no team sports for their children. The reason is that in team sports Andre could just blend in and not stand on his own two feet. These parents prefer individual type sports like golf, tennis, or swimming for their children. *Be Still & Be Quiet* would encourage a strict parent to relax, "take a chill pill" laugh at their own seriousness sometimes, get silly, and recall their own childhood escapades.

On the other side of the fence, team sport parents prefer contact sport and believe that playing baseball, soccer, basketball, football, or hockey will help their children build up their social skills, teach them to be team players, be cooperative, and teach them some leadership skills.

Discuss with your spouse and your child's teacher whether they have observed extra stress in Andre's attitude or behavior. If so, rethink how you communicate with your son. You might want to make changes that will put less pressure and stress on him. A Father's sense of humor in communicating with his son is always a plus.

Whichever you prefer, get involved with your child's abilities, natural talents, and dreams. In furthering your child's education, assist in creating funny computer usernames and passwords. Keep a list of the usernames and passwords in order to protect your child's identify and well-being.

Chapter 25

Develop Social Skills, Good Manners, and Thoughtfulness

Let us review what you have learned about the *Be Still & Be Quiet* method. We have learned that good communication is necessary. We have learned that discipline is a teaching tool designed to stop negative behavior in young children, adolescents, and young adults.

Discipline and structure for your child does not start, let me repeat, does not start in the ninth grade! If you wait to start correcting your child's behavior when she is in her teens, you are too late. You will probably have a teenager who behave in an oppositional-defiant manner, argues with you, and does not listen to you. This is why you start disciplining a one year old by giving directives.

When your child is playing with her toys at home, she must learn to share with siblings, family, and friends. She must cooperate and be willing to pick up toys, books, and other items used in play. Good manners is helping to set dishes on the table or clearing off the table after mealtimes. It would be helpful if the family ate together at the dinner table and at the same time each evening. A thank you prayer to your Lord and Savior could be said by a different family member each night before eating dinner.

Have patience with your three or four year old as she develops the skills to sit at the table, eat with utensils, and say the magic words, "Please, thank you, and you're welcome." Teach your toddler good manners, which include chewing food with her mouth closed and not talking with food in her mouth. When your child burps at the dinner table or burps around strangers, there will be laughter. That is to be expected, but then teach your child to say "Excuse me" or "I'm sorry." Better yet, she should excuse herself before the burp. If possible, she should head toward the bathroom but most definitely get out of the earshot of others.

In learning to clean the table, your toddler can hand you her cup, bowl, and napkin when she is finished and prior to leaving the table. If a young child is taught to say, "Excuse me" when leaving the table, that is a bonus in good manners.

Being structured and orderly with toys and games will add to your child's learned skills of neatness, sharing, and taking turns. You must work consistently on these good manners with your children when they are young if you want to experience fewer embarrassing incidents when they are older.

Imagine your teenage daughter at a nice restaurant with one arm laying on the table as she eats her food with the other hand. It is embarrassing and lacking in manners. Remember as you leave the restaurant to always give lots of praise and hugs for appropriate behavior.

For older children, manners at the table might include a biblical verse recited prior to dinner. Manners would include asking to be excused from the table by saying, "May I be excused?" However, no one should be left at the dinner table to eat alone. Someone should stay there to keep him or her company.

Be Still & Be Quiet does not promote punishment of your teenager that could lead to abuse and physical fights between parent and child. Punishment does not teach. Also, *Be Still & Be Quiet* recommends immediate and fair consequences after bad behavior; however, *Be Still & Be Quiet* does not encourage disciplining your child when you are angry, feeling spiteful, or tired. Sometimes, parents need to take a time-out so they can cool down and not over-react. Your daughter can wait in her room and contemplate her "uncalled for" behavior. *Be*

Still & Be Quiet is about correcting and disciplining your child out of love for her and the life she will live in society.

Be Still & Be Quiet supports parents who teach their child the fifth commandment, "Thou shall honor thy Father and thy Mother." Encourage and praise your daughter when she is obeying this commandment as well as Father God's other nine commandments.

Teach your child to recognize social cues in order to become a team player in life. "Social cues" mean recognizing nonverbal communication, commonly called body language. Body language includes sitting up straight and facing the person talking to you to acknowledge you are paying attention. It calls for good eye contact, but not staring. Another example of good body language is to keep your arms by your side. Arms folded across the chest signal defiance or boredom.

Fathers, teach your young boys to always respect girls and women. Teach family values starting with telling your son to never ever hit or fight a girl. Boys should be taught to open doors and pick up items accidently dropped by females. Some boys and most men are to be commended because they already are opening doors for females when given the opportunity. Picking up dropped items and offering to help a girl or woman in need is not as frequent. Fathers must teach their sons to be gentlemen. Fathers represent strength and loyalty. Your son should have enough confidence to seek you out for advice.

Adolescent girls need their Mothers' coaching on how to become young ladies. A 13 year old girl need to be taught to always dress appropriately when venturing outside the house. She needs to not curse in public or behave in a manner that is disrespectful to her or her family. Etiquette books abound regarding various life experiences and the teaching of manners.

Negative Behavior

Negative behavior takes many forms. The following are a few key examples:

- Your child not wanting to share toys and not interacting nicely with other children due to anger or selfishness
- Hitting someone, not playing fair, or name calling
- Not paying attention to teachers or interrupting grown-ups when they are talking
- Talking back or being disrespectful to an adult
- Being ungrateful and thankless for gifts received from family or friends during the holidays or at a birthday party
- Showing no appreciation when someone does something nice for no apparent reason
- Disrespecting others' belongings or privacy, ownership, or space in the household
- Behaving like a jerk when playing team sports or video games

Introduce your child to proper etiquette. It begins with giving all adults a title; such as, Mr. Moreau, Mrs. Helga, Aunt Christine, Uncle Max, Miss Inez, or Cousin Gabriel. Teach your child to be nice and respectful when older family members want to hug or kiss her. No one wants to experience a child's rude reaction or behavior.

If you constantly allow your young child to interrupt you when you are busy doing something, having a conversation with someone, or talking on the phone, she will in all likelihood grow up to be disruptive, hyperactive, and impatient wherever she goes and with whomever she comes in contact with.. The exception to this is when your child has been taught to say, "Excuse me" and then wait patiently for you to respond to her request.

Teaching etiquette, good manners, and thoughtfulness is an ongoing process at home and at other people's home. For example, when your daughter stays at a relative or friend's home overnight. Upon leaving she would say, "Thank you for having me over." As a parent, your job is to reinforce the practice of being polite. A thank you can be verbal and/or with a thank you card. Sending "Thank you" cards can be an activity done alone or with the help of others in the household. It might help your child learn cursive and not just to be able to print. It is more personal and will be appreciated more than a text message or voicemail.

What about saying thank you to someone living in the home? Yes, of course, otherwise, you will take them for granted and not show appreciation.

Instruct your child to always knock on a closed door and get permission before entering a bedroom that is not hers. Also, once inside the room, she is never to touch, borrow, or take things from a family member without permission.

If something borrowed becomes damaged or broken, the responsible child must make every effort to replace or pay for the property even to a sibling, "no," especially to a sibling. Teach your child good manners and she will have healthy boundaries.

To develop privacy, boundaries, and space at home, a fun activity for families could be to design doorknob hangers, create door signs, or decorate each bedroom door in a fun and unique way.

When it comes to sports and video games, consistently teach your child the social skill of playing by the rules and interacting well with siblings and peers. Do not allow name calling, bullying, or fighting ever! If your child is playing with a younger sibling, monitor their activities to ensure she plays fair and allows the little ones a chance to shine with a win sometimes.

Explain the role of good sportsmanship and being a team player. If you have time, research with your daughter an afterschool sport or wholesome activity that she like; such as, softball, soccer, basketball, tennis, and skateboarding. Wholesome activities might include: studying art or drawing, writing poetry and entering contests, or taking piano lessons, which might bring out the best of her many talents. Additionally, she can volunteer and participate in community leadership and self-awareness programs for children. Parents must realize that not all children have athletic skills and that is okay.

Chapter 26

Teaching Children Manners
Continues-Ages 7 to 10

When your child starts a new school year, you should have already discussed your expectations of him on the school grounds and in the classroom. Among your expectations are that your child will raise his hand before speaking in the classroom or as instructed by the teacher. He will not interrupt you and the teacher talking unless permission to speak is granted after an "Excuse me" request has been made to one or both adults. Your child will then wait for a respond.

When did children learn not to speak to adults as they walk past them? Probably, it came from the teaching, "Do not talk to strangers." and "Stranger danger." For safety, this is so true, such is the world we live in today!

Parents, you can model good listening skills and good eye contact to show that you are paying attention and have not allowed yourself to be distracted. For your shy child, instruct him on the following exercise that might help him to make new friends. He should get into the habit of shaking the newly introduced person's hand and saying their names often in conversation until he has memorized the name. Your child can practice this with his siblings and friends or even role playing with a stuffed animal until he gets used to this exercise for memorizing names.

Chapter 27

Teaching Preteens and Teenagers to Be Good Guests

A parent of a preteen or teenager who ask to stay over at a friend's house for a weekend sleepover should review negative behaviors they want their child to reframe from when visiting. The following are examples:

- Being loud with a "do not care" attitude, swearing, poor table manners, rolling eyes when asked to do something, and other forms of disrespect to the host family
- Overstaying your welcome by not knowing when to go home
- Not cleaning up after yourself
- Not keeping in touch with your own family during your visit
- Not saying thank you or showing gratitude to the hosts prior to going home

A parent has to instill in your adolescent child your expectations for her behavior when not in your presence. Your child will not always do what she knows is right. Sometimes, she will prefer to please her peers; but, if you have taught her to be respectful at all times, not just sometimes, she will usually not disappoint you. This is where early and consistent discipline pays off.

You must continue to parent and instruct your child when to come home or when to check in with a call or a text. It is not her decision. It is your decision. If you are indecisive and easily persuaded to change your mind, you are setting yourself up for problems.

Years later, you will find yourself telling Isis to come home as she is told. What happens next is a heated argument because she wants to manipulate you and tell you what she wants to do as she usually does. Because Isis is now a teenager, she might become physically combative when she finally does come home from a sleepover. Never let your child put her hands on you. If you need to, have her arrested and taken to juvenile for assault. This is called, "tough love," which is sometimes necessary when dealing with an out-of-control child.

Your child should never be allowed to tell you when she will be home except in an emergency situation. Do not allow your child to ever disrespect you by cursing you or by failing to tell you of her comings and goings. Failure by your child to do as expected is cause for grounding, loss of privileges, and takeaways. Do not allow your daughter to simply walk out the front door and you see her when she returns. "Oh heck no!" When Isis is grown and has her own place, then she may choose not to tell you of her activities or her comings and goings.

Mantra #4: Not in My House; or, My House, My Rules

Here are some dos and don'ts when communicating with your tween and teenage child:

- Establish eye contact to indicate your interest
- Validate your child's right to speak openly and calmly.
- Be patient and allow your child to be goofy and silly at times, humor is good
- Listen without judging or putting importance on past actions.
- Moderate your voice to match what you want to say and how you want it heard.
- Listen to understand rather than listening to respond.

Chapter 28

Young Adults on Their Way to Adulthood Ages 13 – 18

This section works best as a joint venture between parent and teenager. It is serious and important. It is a challenge for both of you to see if indeed unacceptable behaviors are starting to occur. If you have a weekly meeting time in your household, this is a good time to discuss any problematic behavior listed below. If your teenager is exhibiting none of the negative behaviors below, "Congratulations, your parenting style and skills are excellent."

Let us direct the attention in this session to issues of ugliness and negative behaviors that need to be addressed by the both of you for satisfactory solutions. Consider the following:

- Disrespecting your Mother or Father by not listening, talking back, cursing at them, and walking away or running away.
- Arguing about the cellphone, not getting off the cellphone when told to, and not handing over the cellphone when instructed to do so.
- Blowing off your parent's directive by being late and changing everybody's plans.
- Being rude by playing loud, obscene music; or, wearing headphones or talking on the cellphone when you are supposed

to be talking with your Mother who has asked for your full attention.

- Dressing provocatively particularly when she is just 13 years old.
- A daughter wearing too much makeup.
- Having a bad attitude.
- Wearing gang attire or saggy clothes and having gang paraphernalia in your bedroom.
- Hanging with new, negative, or much older friends who might be high school dropouts.
- Smoking cigarettes, vapers, or marijuana; drinking alcohol, drug use and/or abuse.

When you are having a discussion with your son or daughter, do not compete with loud music, headphones, computers, or cellphones after instructing your child to get off the phone, turn off the music, or take off the headphones. After this discussion with your teenager, serious changes as needed should be implemented immediately. Should the discussion become heated, call for calm and quiet. Hopefully, it will not be necessary to push back with groundings, takeaways, or ultimatums. Be prepared, however, to make the hard decision and implement consequences to resolve issues and stop any negative, disruptive behavior which is causing pain and panic within the household.

Here is a situation that may not be enforceable but is worth mentioning to your teenager. *Be Still & Be Quiet* places a high importance on connectedness with other people. As the world becomes more detached and accelerated with individual activities and less connectedness with family, friends, and other people, what can be done about it? Here is one thing older teens and young adults can do, and again, it is about manners. It encourages all people to be role models of courtesy and kindness.

If you are walking down the street listening to music on your headphones. As you approach another person, good manners dictate that you look the person in the eyes and greet them; or, at the very least nod your head up or down towards him or her to acknowledge their presence. This is a gesture of connectedness and friendliness. Your ears are busy listening to the music, but there is nothing stopping your head from nodding, a form of nonverbal communication. To take it one step further, it would be so nice if folks once again spoke to each other as they meet at gas stations, grocery stores, banks, walking down the street, and in general when out and about. If they don't return your salutation, it is okay because your kind gesture would "pay it forward" throughout the day.

What would help this sad predicament of not speaking to your fellow man today? I'm glad you asked. You might want to organize a "speak to your neighbor" block party; a "speak to all" in my neighborhood day; or, a national, "speak to anyone and everyone," month long movement! What do you think of the idea?

This same scenario plays out when you enter a room with other people in the room. Good manners dictate that you communicate first with a friendly hello, a smile, or maybe a little wave to those already present.

60 Values and Skills Every Child Should Master before High School

1. Pray and believe in a higher power.
2. Respect yourself in all situations.
3. Respect authority figures.
4. Respect adults.
5. Respect your peers.
6. Work with your teacher and set goals for success.
7. Disagree without being disagreeable.
8. Say "No" gracefully.
9. Master your emotions.
10. Walk away from arguments.
11. Sort, wash, and iron your own clothes.
12. Dress appropriately for formal and casual events.

13. Read the newspaper daily.
14. Use the dictionary.
15. Use a thesaurus.
16. Be a good listener.
17. Set the table for meals.
18. Learn how to read a map.
19. Read a bus or train schedule.
20. Take a bus using a transfer slip
21. Apply for summer employment.
22. Keep your room clean.
23. Recite a daily prayer.
24. Understand the King's English versus slang.
25. Choose proper English rather than profanity.
26. Understand formal dining etiquette.
27. Properly use eating utensils.
28. Order from a menu.
29. Learn CPR.
30. Babysit younger siblings.
31. Deal correctly with jealousy.
32. Hail a taxi in the big city.
33. Arrange a pickup by Uber or Lyft using apps.
34. Be a team player.
35. Be truthful.
36. Resolve conflict nonviolently.
37. Attend school regularly without incident.
38. Pick friends who complement your life.
39. Honor family values and moral teachings.
40. Send thank-you notes.
41. Research and use library reference material.
42. Shake hands firmly.
43. Establish & maintain good eye contact when talking with someone.
44. Navigate safely on social media sites.
45. Eat healthy and exercise daily.

46. Clean your room and the bathroom the right way.
47. Mop a floor & vacuum the carpet regularly.
48. Check on a senior citizen, relative, or neighbor.
49. Check on a family member or friend in the hospital.
50. Open the door for adults, especially ladies and seniors.
51. Be able to name city officials, as well as, city and state politicians.
52. Be able to name the four US time zones.
53. Be able to name the fifty states and their capitals.
54. Be able to name the five Great Lakes.
55. Make your junior high school honor roll.
56. Open a bank account and know how to write a check.
57. Properly answer the telephone and take messages.
58. Read and understand labels on food.
59. Cut the grass and rake the leaves.
60. Appreciate your family and all they do for you.

Chapter 29

Teenagers Have Responsibilities

If your child is 16 to 18, you might give him the privilege of staying up until 10:00 pm, if he wants, on weeknights based on his school performance and help around the house. The TV would go off or be off limits for younger children. Your teen's homework must be completed during the week and checked by you before he receives any late night privileges. Some children will claim to have completed homework at school, but you should verify that.

After he finishes his homework, encourage your son to read a book, a physical book. Nothing in the 21ˢᵗ century will ever take the place of a physical book, the smell, the sound of pages flipping, the feel of it whether new, or, worn from long term use. Your child will usually do what is required of him and no more. The bottom line is a child who loves to read is a gifted child. A child should learn to love reading early in life and with set aside reading time and consistency, you can make it happen.

A child's room is never off limits. His room can be randomly searched for gang clothing and paraphernalia that are not allowed at home or school. Look for any signs your child is experimenting with drugs. You want to be informed by monitoring any changes in your child's behavior; new, bad boy friends; low performance at school; and sneaking offensive and/or illegal items into the home.

If you are consistent, you are in charge all the time, not some of the time. Do not allow your child to parent himself. When a child parent himself, he does what he want, when he want, and how he want. He will disrespect you by not listening and not obeying your house rules. Your child does not tell you what he is going to do, he asks. When your son gets too big to listen and obey your rules, "tough love" is needed to keep a stable and orderly household. He might need to leave your home that night! Like right now! He will not be allowed back until he is ready to apology, listen, obey, and respect your decisions.

Use mantra # 4, "My house, my rules," as often as necessary. If you enforce this in a loving manner, in your loving home, your child might not like what is being told to him but he will understand, accept, and respect the reason for it being said. Life is such that as children and adults, we do not always like what authority figures ask or even tell us to do. Thus the phrase, "No man is an island." This phrase suggest we find ways to get along, to live in a civilized and orderly world, to follow the rules, and often times to "Just Do It." When possible, use humor with your child. Sometimes a code word can be decided upon and used between you two to relieve a tense situation. It might be "bootsy" or "whatup." It will be whatever you two agree upon that will always cause you both to laugh. It is your code word. You might want to burst into a song during an angry episode. It is guaranteed to put a smile on your child's face and your face, especially if you happen to be a really good singer.

Take this scenario, a responsible young adult son with a driver's license who is driving his parent's car and on his parent's insurance would never dream of purposely running a red light. Would he? If he did, it could mean jeopardizing his life, his passenger's life, and possibly another driver's life should he hit a car in the intersection. Of course not, due to him thinking about his parents, his self, and caring about other drivers on the road.

On the other hand, an irresponsible, out-of-control, disrespectful adult child might run a red light jeopardizing so many lives due to

Chapter 30

Parenting as in Parenthood

Children who are close to their parents are less likely to engage in risky behavior. The more involved parents are in their children's lives, the more valued they will feel and the more likely they will stay close to their parents physically, emotionally, and spiritually as they grow into adulthood.

PlayStations and video games are time killers with no instructional value. This is worth repeating. Video games with overuse can become addictive. And, little ones watching cartoons on TV for hours will make some youngsters hyperactive. Indeed, TV shows, PlayStations, and video games stimulate the brain so that a child will run, hop, jump, bounce off the wall and possibly be overly talkative, inattentive, and hyperactive.

In contrast, a calm house is one in which the TV is turned off during the day from time to time for quiet time and to allow for productive time, music lessons, board games, puzzles, pet care, and gardening. As explained in chapter 22, "Less Clutter Equals Less Stress," a calm house is one in which children are taught to play quietly. One way of making this happen is to designate a device free area in the home and also a quiet time for reading, studying, and participating in quiet activities. An hour or two prior to bedtime would be a good designated time for calm and quiet. Do not be so strict that you do not have the flexibility during the week to grant permission for a special TV show during the usual quiet time.

Family praying at the dinner table

Eat together as often as you can. Meals are great opportunities to talk about the day's events, to unwind, and to bond. Try to make it happen at least four times a week.

When your son prepares to leave the house, do not hesitate to ask where is he going, with whom, and what will they be doing. If he will be visiting someone's home, ask if there will be an adult there. Get to know your child's friends and their parents so you will be familiar with their family values, activities, and interests. If they have guns in their homes for protection, you need to know that.

Children 11 to 13, or even 15 years old still crave structure and guidance, so show them you care by setting limits. Tell your child to call you at a designated time during an activity or event outside the home.

When your son starts going to parties, do not hesitate to call and talk to the parent at the party house. On party night, do not be embarrassed to drop by to say, "Hello" and make sure adult supervision is in place.

To a Mother who has a daughter going to a party, your daughter does not need you to be her BFF. She does not need a home girl. She needs a Mother to teach her to say, "No" to an inappropriate question and to leave quickly during an uncomfortable situation. Parenting is a full time job to be taken seriously.

> A father must make one-on-one
> quality time with his son in order to
> build a relationship of trust and love.

A Father who puts an earring in his son's ear and calls him "Little man" has a tendency to project an older age for his toddler. This same Father might easily dismiss his child's antics and the sassing of adults. Your child will grow up soon enough. So Dad, please do not hurry him up and spoil his childhood. Allow your child to be a child as long as possible.

To a Father who has a teenage son, your son does not need you to be his homeboy. He does not need his Father to introduce him to females. He does not need you to show him how to be a macho man who never cries, drinks beer, smokes marijuana, and scores big with women. What he need is a Father who is a positive and responsible role model. Additional, your son needs to see his Father with a job or a self-employed business. A Father who is the families' breadwinner. Your son needs to see the respectful way in which you talk to and treat your wife, his Mother, and other women.

Be Still & be Quiet advises Father's to make sure you are not guilty of bullying your children. They have a right to be free of any form of abuse. That being said, tough talk is sometimes needed to reestablish control. A reminder is sometimes needed regarding house rules and your teenager's responsibility to obey those rules. Your child should be willing to adhere to your rules if your relationship has been built on trust and the well-being of all in the family.

Fathers should know that daughters have a special, opposite sex type of hold on them. Mothers should know that sons have a special, opposite sex type of hold on them. That is a fact of Mother Nature.

In a troublesome relationship between parent, child, and/or siblings, you might need family counseling. Family counseling is helpful and at its best when all in the household agree that outside, professional involvement is needed.

The entire family must be willing to actively listen with an open mind and be willing to perform homework assignments and journaling as instructed by the counselor in order to bring about positive change.

Counseling can help with improved communication skills, decreased depression, less stress, less drama, headaches, arguments, and tension within the home. Counseling helps with so many issues affecting family member's interactions with each other. It could be from poor communication skills, misunderstandings, mistreatment, and cursing at each other. Counseling might be able to resolve dislikes, a lack of patience, no cooperation, jealousy, and disrespectful treatment by a family member.

Your child might be willing to consult with a youth minister assuming you are a church family that has prayed together but is now going through difficult times.

Despite your best job of being a good parent, if peers, gangs, alcohol, or drugs have influenced your 15 to 18 year-old negatively, you will notice a difference in attitude and behavior. If your child is becoming increasingly disrespectful, argumentative, talking back, will not listen, will not follow the rules, is defiant and oppositional, and is making poor choices daily, you might have to show him the front door. This is called, "tough love." It could be based on safety for all in your home or for peace of mind. Packing clothes and putting your teenager out of the home for out-of-control behavior, threats, and fights, could become necessary as a last resort.

If your child talks grown and acts grown, let him live as a grown-up but somewhere else. Do not accept or live with verbal, physical, or emotional abuse. Do not allow outsiders, who mean well, to influence your decision and treatment of your son. Do not accept a guilt trip that your child or others may attempt to burden and confuse you with; when, in fact, your child has made your decision necessary. Remember, "My house, my rules."

It will be hard to put your son out of the house, but do not give in when you are right, and do not give up on your child whom you love. Know that things will probably get worse before they get better. One solution is to pray. Pray often for a covenant of protection from God over your child. Pray that your son's out-of-control behavior will stop when he ask for the Lord's grace and mercy and humble his self. Not until then will he come to the realization that there is no place like home and especially a good home.

In the meantime, be prepared should your child's attitude and behavior become worse. Your son might say, "I am my own person. You cannot tell me what to do." If putting your child out of the home sounds too extreme, you might be able to show him a modified version of tough love by sending him to a willing grandmother or aunt who has a good relationship with him. If your son wants to return home, he has to show that through his improved behavior and attitude. Be sure family members are comfortable and always safe with this arrangement.

Do not enable your teenage child by making excuses for why he misbehaves. His disobedience is not because he is doing the best he can. Know that he is making choices, not doing things blindly with no thought given to his actions. Maybe he chooses to live a non-traditional lifestyle that conflicts with yours. Maybe he sees your salary from a job as too slow. He wants big money and he wants it now. This is called, "instant gratification."

If your son is not on medication, he alone is responsible for his choices and his actions. His defiance, negativity, and bad attitude will cause him problems at home, at school, in the community, and the outside world. His disrespect of the home often spills over into breaking the law, arrests, and court proceedings. This often comes from trying to make quick money by committing crimes, or having multiple run-ins and arrests by law enforcement.

Parents, childhood goes by so quickly. Do spend as much time as possible with your child or children and instill in them your family values, ethics, morals, compassion, confidence, self-esteem, self-respect, and respect for others. Family values and integrity starts in the home. It keeps all in the household feeling happy, secure, and safe.

Chapter 31

Do Parents Need to
Be Still & Be Quiet?

Be Still & Be Quiet suggests that yes, couples need to take care of themselves by being still and quiet as well. Husbands and wives need to talk to each other softly, kindly, and lovingly. Remember, you are best friends to the end.

The best relationship is one in which your love for each other is greater than your need for each other. In long lasting marriages, some wives have said, "If your husband loves you more than you love him, you are a very lucky woman indeed." A single parent needs downtime as well. Treat yourself to goodness: a good time, a good meal, and good companionship.

Sometimes, couples have to compromise when they disagree on how to discipline their child. Early on in your relationship, there should have been a discussion and an understanding on the need to agree to disagree.

When angry with your spouse about how best to discipline your child, do so in private and away from "frightened eyes" and "big ears."

Are you overstimulated, over engaged, overwhelmed, and overcommitted? Sometimes, parents have schedules that are too busy. You could be on too many committees; belong to too many organizations; or, have too many outside of the home responsibilities.

Like children, parents can also have too many techno-gadgets in their lives. This can result in negative, angry, and impatient behavior just like your child.

Suppose it is your turn to take your toddler to the park to spend quality time together as you watch and supervise her play. Instead you are talking on your cell or checking your text messages. Distracted parents who do not disconnect from their cell phone run the risk of sending the message to their young child that they are not as important. A Yale University study shows a 10% increase in children getting hurt at parks and at home when iPhones initially came out for sale. Checking your text messages 40 or 50 times a day is being called, "Techno Referencing."

Additionally, parents are often stressed out by absurd amounts of email, unrealistic deadlines, budget cuts, gossiping coworkers, discriminating supervisors, or an aging body that does not want to cooperate with the mind. You could benefit from *Be Still & Be Quiet* as well.

As a couple, you will need to practice and strengthen your love for each other. One way to keep your love alive is to have a "date night." You can do this by hiring a babysitter and taking a trip out of town; or, you make a reservation at a nearby motel in town. Children are not allowed. The exception would be a newborn baby.

At the motel, work on falling in love all over again. To all lovers, turn your partner on like you used to. Be sexy, think sexy, and believe in yourself. Believe that you can do it. When you succeed, your love life will be strengthened physically, mentally, and spiritually. Maybe it is the way your wife wears her hair that entices you. Could it be he looks sexy in his new pajamas?

If you and your spouse do not have a sexy bone in your body due to becoming overweight, a joint gym membership may be the answer. It will not work if you do not go. Imagine if the two of you, lose weight, achieve higher self-esteem, feel good and look sexy. Then, you owe it to yourselves to "Party Like It's 2025!" How cool is that! Ha, ha!

Husbands, provide for your wife and children, be the breadwinner.

If she has a bigger salary then you, it is okay because to all wives, you are not in competition with your husband. You are his helpmate. Trust in him and allow him to lead the family.

Parents need to celebrate with just the two of you all of your accomplishments as good parents. Couple counselors encourage and explain the benefits that couples gain from a "date night" once a month or most definitely every two months. Date nights are where you two reconnect and work on your relationship. If you can go out of town, that is even better. Put family and home life on a back burner until you return. You might need to keep in touch with the babysitter or family member babysitting in case an emergency occurs. Please, do put effort and planning into your reconnection as lovers and as a couple.

Read the following and extrapolate what you want from what was written by Regina Brett, who lives in Cleveland, Ohio.

45 Lessons Life Taught Me
Regina Brett

1. Life isn't fair, but it is still good.
2. When in doubt, just take the next small step.
3. Life is too short to waste time hating anyone.
4. Your job won't take care of you when you are sick. Your friends and parents will. Stay in touch.
5. Pay off your credit cards every month.
6. You don't have to win every argument. Agree to disagree.
7. Cry with someone. It is more healing than crying alone.
8. It is okay to get angry with God. He can take it.
9. Save for retirement starting with your first paycheck.
10. When it comes to chocolate, resistance is futile.
11. Make peace with your past so it will not screw up the present.
12. It is okay to let your children see you cry.
13. Do not compare your life with others. You have no idea what their journey is all about.
14. If your relationship has to be a secret, you shouldn't be in it.

15. Everything can change in the blink of an eye, but don't worry. God never blinks.
16. Take a deep breath. It calms the mind.
17. Get rid of anything that isn't useful, beautiful, or joyful.
18. Whatever doesn't kill you really does make you stronger.
19. It's never too late to have a happy childhood, but the second one is up to you and no one else.
20. When it comes to going after what you love in life, don't take no for an answer.
21. Burn the fancy candles, sleep on the nice sheets, eat off the good china, and wear your fancy lingerie. Do not save them for a special occasion. Today is special.
22. Over prepare then go with the flow.
23. Be eccentric now. Don't wait for old age to wear purple.
24. The most important sex organ is the brain.
25. No one is in charge of your happiness but you.
26. Frame every so-called disaster with this question, "In 5 years, will this matter?"
27. Always choose life.
28. Forgive everyone everything.
29. What other people think of you is none of your business.
30. Time heals almost everything. Give time, time.
31. However good or bad a situation is, it will change.
32. Do not take yourself so seriously, no one else does.
33. Believe in miracles.
34. God loves you because of who God is, not because of anything you did or didn't do.
35. Do not audit life. Show up and make the most of it now.
36. Growing old beats the alternative, which is dying young.
37. Your children get only one childhood.
38. All that truly matters in the end is that you loved.
39. Get outside every day. Miracles are waiting everywhere.
40. If we all threw our problems in a pile and saw everyone else's problems, we'd be quick to grab ours back.

41. Envy is a waste of time. You already have everything that you need.
42. The best is yet to come.
43. No matter how you feel, get up, get dressed, and show up.
44. Yield the right of way.
45. Life isn't tied with a bow, but it is still a gift.

It is a blessing from God is to have an obedient child, especially a teenager who is exceptional at home and at school. A teenager with a prideful sense of citizenship and all that it entails. As his parent, you will want to encourage his good manners, respect for himself, and for others. It is a joy if he is dressing appropriately and using electronic devices in a manner that adheres to your house rules.

You are further blessed if your child receives excellent grades and plans to attend a trade school or get a college degree before going into the work force. From time to time, your family may want to celebrate love and respect for each other for enduring all the hard work in maintaining healthy relationships and for maintaining real and meaningful ethics and family values.

When did your success as parents start? It started with the discipline, corrections, and guidelines *Be Still & Be Quiet* recommended and encouraged you to use during toddlerhood with your child. Ideally, *Be Still & Be Quiet*'s advice continued with your child's upbringing during elementary school, junior high, until graduation from high school, onward to a four year university or a vocational certificate; and, finally, on to a successful adult life. You are now the expert in your household. Please keep doing what works for you and your family.

Below is a quiz for parents. Copy it! Refer to it daily, weekly, or as often as needed. Add questions that fit your need. Rewrites are encouraged.

1. What am I feeling today? Explain.
2. How was my week? Describe it.
3. What does being happy mean to me?

4. What would make me happy?
5. Do I support, make time for, show compassion to, and communicate well with my child?
6. Am I a good listener to my child?
7. Am I a good role model to my child regarding our family values and integrity?
8. Do I frequently give in to my child after saying "No?"
9. Being a Mother is a blessing because _____

   _____.

10. Being a Father is a blessing because _____

    _____.

Here is a final thought. For years, society has been telling God to get out of its schools, public events, even out of our lives. And being the God He is, I believe that He has agreed to do just that. Ask yourself this question, *"How can the United States expect God to give it His blessings and protection if we demand He leave us alone?"* Therefore, we reap what we sow.

I guarantee this book will be controversial due to its no nonsense style of parenting. This is a good thing because we all need more dialogue on parenting. Since a no-nonsense style of parenting is the principal idea of this book, *Be Still & Be Quiet* is not for everyone. The hope is that it will be beneficial to you in one way or another. Of course, there is no cookie-cutter, one-size-fits-all when raising children. Most everyone would agree that some children are strong-minded, hard-headed, and some seem hell-bent on being bad and troublesome. That being said, many new parents and single Mothers are in need of advice, counseling, and mentoring.

Be Still & Be Quiet is designed primarily to address solutions to early childhood rearing in order to diminish or eliminate future problems. The mission here is to get you to start early and be consistent with disciplining your child. Should you need mental health services for your son or daughter, get in touch with the National Alliance on Mental Illness (NAMI; www.nami.org/aka) and the Office of Minority Health (http://minorityhealth.hhs.gov/omh/browse.aspx)?

That is it. Congratulations! You have completed *Be Still & Be Quiet*. Good luck to you with your child or children and to all your future endeavors!

> *I can do all things through the power of God which strengthens me.*
> —Philippians 4:13

References

Battle Hymn of the Tiger Mother by Amy Chua, A Penguin Books, Manhattan, NY, 2011

The Baby College by the Harlem's Children's Zone (best-practice program), Harlem, NY, 2000

What to Do … When Kids Are Mean to Your Child by Elin McCoy, Pleasantville, NY, Reader's Digest, 1997

The Hair-Raising Joys of Raising Boys by Dave Meurer, Ada, MI, Revell Publishing, 2006

Grateful Kids by Jeffrey J. Froh and Giacomo Bono, Conshohocken, PA, Templeton Press, 2015

The Enabler: When Helping Hurts the Ones You Love by Angelyn Miller, Nashville, TN, Hunter House Publishers, 1988

Simplicity Parenting: Using the Extraordinary Power of Less to Raise Calmer, Happier, and More Secure Kids by Kim John Payne, M.Ed, with Lisa M. Ross, New York, Ballantine Books, 2009

Don't Sweat the Small Stuff by Richard Carlson, Westport, CT, Hyperion, 1997

Their Name Is Today by Johann Arnold, New York, Plough Publishing House, 2014

All I Really Need to Know I Learned in Kindergarten by Robert Fulghum, Penguin Random House, 2003

Go the F—k to Sleep by Adam Mansbach, Brooklyn, New York City, NY, Akashic Books, 2011

Laying Down the Law by Dr. Ruth Peters, Harlan, IA, Rodale Press, 2002

Who Moved My Cheese? by Spencer Johnson, MD, New York City, NY, G.P. Putnam's Sons, 1998

We are the Change We Seek: the Speeches of Barack Obama by E.J. Dionne, New York City, NY, Bloomsbury Publishing, 2017

Future Shock by Alvin Toffler, New York, Bantam Books, 1971

The Vanishing American Adult by Benjamin Sasse, Manhattan, NY, St. Martin's press, 2017

Surprise Ride (SR) creative toys & activities, surpriseride.com

Fresno Economic Opportunities Commission (EOC) www.fresnoEOC. org/headstart

waituntil8th@gmail.com

About the Author

R. Mikki Addison is a motivational speaker, community activist, mental health counselor, and social worker. As a motivational speaker, she has a special interest in issues pertaining to women, girls, and teenagers.

Mikki McIntosh-Addison graduated from Thomas A. Edison High School in Fresno, California. She graduated from California State University, Fresno (CSUF) in 1987 with a BA in communication and worked at Channel 47 for several years in studio production. She received her Master's Degree in Social Work (MSW) in 1995 from CSUF.

With her MSW degree in hand, Mrs. Addison was employed from 1995 until 1999 by Positive Attitude Outlook, (FFA) a foster family agency, as a social worker for children placed in court-ordered foster homes. She assisted with family relationship building, stress reduction, reviewed money allotments, transported children from schools during crises interventions, and to psychiatric appointments.

In 1999, Mrs. Addison was hired by Fresno County Behavioral Health as a Mental Health Counselor. She worked at the Fresno County Jail for 7-1/2 years as a member of the Jail Psychiatrist Services team. She provided crisis intervention, stabilization, and individual and group counseling. She initiated California Code, WIC 5150 holds which takes an individual involuntary into protective custody due to being a danger to self, a danger to others, or gravely disabled. The patient is transported by law enforcement to a hospital or psychiatric facility for a 72 hour psychiatric evaluation.

In 2008, Mrs. Addison transferred to the Juvenile Justice Campus (JJC) as a Mental Health Counselor. She counseled male and female minors on the detention side of the campus waiting to go to court. Additionally, she counseled minor on the commitment side of the campus having been found guilty as charged. Mrs. Addison stayed at the JJC until 2014, when she retired from her employment with Fresno County.

Mrs. Addison is the owner of *For the Inside* (FTI). She is designer of stylish, fashionable T-shirts. She is the photographer for a line of God's creation postcards. Additionally, FTI creates greeting cards featuring original artwork by inmates.

Mrs. Addison served as President of the West Fresno Democratic Club (WFDC) from 2007 to 2017. She was a member of the Fresno County Democratice Central Committee (FCDCC) during this same period in time.

Mrs. Addison is a member of Sisters in Crime, a mystery writers' book club.

She received the 2012 and 2018 Special Recognition Award from Black Women Organized for Political Action (BWOPA) honoring her community activist work.

For book signing and speaking engagements, contact Mrs. Addison at her email address, fortheinside@hotmail.com; or, fortheinside.com.

Printed in the United States
By Bookmasters